WRITING

THIRD EDITION

Phyllis Dutwin, M.A.
President, Dutwin Associates
Training and Development Programs
North Kingstown, Rhode Island
and

Harriet Diamond, M.A.
President, Diamond Associates
Multi-Faceted Training and Development
Westfield, New Jersey

BARRON'S

All inquiries should be addressed to:
Barron's Educational Series, Inc.
250 Wireless Boulevard
Hauppauge, NY 11788
http://www.barronseduc.com

Library of Congress Catalog Card No. 99-046423

International Standard Book No. 0-7641-1206-6

Library of Congress Cataloging-in-Publication Data

Dutwin, Phyllis.
    Writing the easy way / Phyllis Dutwin and Harriet Diamond.—3rd ed.
        p.   cm.—(The easy way)
    Originally published: 1985.
        Includes bibliographical references.
        ISBN 0-7641-1206-6
        1. English language—Rhetoric.   2. English language—Grammar.
    3. Business writing.   4. Report writing.   I. Title.   II. Series.
    III. Diamond, Harriet.
PE1408.D87   2000
808'.042 21—dc21   99-046423
                                                CIP

PRINTED IN THE UNITED STATES OF AMERICA
9 8 7 6 5 4 3 2 1

Table of Contents _____

Dedication

This book is dedicated to those adults who did not enjoy English
courses in high school, did not major in English in college,
and sought careers that did not require writing proficiency, but
now must incorporate writing into their daily activities.

Acknowledgments

The authors thank these copyright owners for permission to reprint portions of the following works:

American Phonemeter Corp., for the paragraph on page 85, from their 1982 Annual Report.

Consumers Union, Inc., for the paragraph on page 83, adapted from "Sunscreens," *Consumers Reports* June 1983.

Burrows, William E., for the paragraph on page 80. First appeared in *Science Digest* © by The Hearst Corporation.

Davis, William S., for the paragraph on page 86, from *BASIC: Getting Started*, © 1981. Published by Addison-Wesley Publishing Company.

Diamond Associates for portions of *Effective Business Writing*.

Malcolm, Andrew, for paragraph 5 on page 82. Copyright © 1990 by The New York Times Company. Reprinted by permission.

Smithsonian Books, for the paragraph on page 80, from *Thread of Life*. © 1982 by Smithsonian Institution Press.

The authors extend special thanks to Ellen Diamond for her contribution to the second edition, and to Linda Diamond for her extensive revisions to the third edition.

Introduction

You care about your appearance; therefore, you pay some attention to your clothes and your hair. Your physical appearance is part of the image you want to project. Your writing also projects an image of you. Be sure it represents you well. Each time you send a letter, write a memo, or hand in a term paper, you are on display. If written material does not leave your desk until you've taken the time to style your sentences and correct any grammar and usage errors, you will appear educated and effective.

Business managers frequently complain that employees do not know how to write. Depending upon the clarity of the writing, a report or memo can confuse rather than inform. Managers obviously don't want to spend too much time correcting written work; more frustrating is time spent rewriting or making follow-up calls to clarify. Extra time spent on your end to make your writing clear and correct saves everyone time in the end.

Business managers are not the only people concerned about the quality of writing today. Teachers say that students have problems expressing their understanding of a subject simply because they cannot write about it. The difference between getting one grade or another, or even passing or failing a course, may depend on being able to answer an essay question or prepare a term paper.

Even when writing is a personal matter between family members or friends, a letter of instruction to a repairperson, or a complaint to a department store, your writing will represent you. If your letter is sloppy or your meaning unclear, you risk making the wrong impression— or not getting what you want.

What does this mean for you? Everything. If you communicate well, you are more likely to be hired, to earn better grades, and to have your wants understood. In short, if you are able to communicate clearly and effectively through your writing, you will be more likely to succeed at whatever you do.

How Can This Book Help? _____

Throughout their schooling, many people have had to write, have been graded on writing, but have not been taught *how* to write. For example, if, by the time you reached the fifth grade you were still adding a column of 5's to find out how much seven of them equaled, a teacher would have insisted that you learn the multiplication tables. You would have been shown a procedure for calculating the answer in a short time. You would have suffered a bit while you learned to multiply, but afterwards you would have had a process that cut your working time while giving you more confidence and less pain.

This book is designed to give you a process to apply to writing, to help you get your thoughts on paper. "Stop!" you say. "I don't even have the thoughts to put on paper. Can you help me, too?" You do, in fact, have thoughts to put on paper, but when confronted with a blank sheet, those thoughts often retreat. Relax; you are not alone. Even professional writers experience problems with their writing.

Writing the Easy Way is designed to help you combat the "empty paper syndrome" with tips on collecting those thoughts and arranging them in a meaningful way. This book will teach you how to reduce the time it takes to write (from creation to revision) and, in so doing, will help rid you of some of the frustration. If you don't like the way you write, if writing is a painful process, stop blaming yourself. Stop suffering. Learn to write, THE EASY WAY.

1.

Think Before You Write _____

Whatever you intend to write, whether it be a letter or a term paper, one thing is certain. You should make some important decisions before you get started. You could delay making those decisions—as many people do—and end up writing your piece again and again until you hit upon what you want to say. Or you could do some critical thinking *before* you write and save yourself a great deal of time and frustration. Which way is better? Try our way this time and see whether you like the results.

Some Basic Questions

What are the questions you should ask yourself before you write? Let's consider them, and see how the answers to them will make your writing easier.

Should I Write?

If you can accomplish your purpose by talking to someone, then talk! During your work day, if you see an associate three, four, perhaps five times, there may be no need to write a memo regarding a simple matter. Say what you want if the issue can be concluded by speaking, and save time and paper. However, don't expect a busy co-worker to carry a request or message in his or her head for an hour, a day, or a week. Do yourself and the person with whom you are communicating a favor. Write the question, give the information, or make the request you want; otherwise, you risk having your message ignored, forgotten, or misunderstood.

If you are a homeowner with a complaint about the broken street light on your corner, your request to have it fixed will get faster attention if it arrives on paper. As a student with an assignment to write a term paper, of course you have no choice but to put your thoughts down on paper. The teacher wants to know how well you have learned your subject but also wishes to see how effectively you can organize that information and convey it to another person. When you write, you must make your thoughts clear to your reader. Thus, in many situations, you will have to write your message, and you want that message to be understood.

Who Is Your Audience?

You can't begin writing until you establish who will read what you write. Your audience will determine what type of writing you will do. Think of one idea going to two different people. For example, the following two letters describe a job, first to a friend, then to a potential employer. Notice how Theresa's tone changes, depending on whether she is writing to someone she knows well or to a potential employer.

April 3, 2000

Dear Maria,

I've finally decided to pack in this dead-end job. I can no longer calmly listen to Mr. B. present my ideas as his accomplishments. He is so convinced they're his, he even brags to me about them. Most recently, I developed a training program for new employees. I sent him a draft. A week later, a manual was circulated with his name on it. He didn't even correct my typing error. I've applied for a comparable position in another company and hope to have good news for you soon.

Love,
Theresa

---

16 Sunset Road
Boise, Idaho 83701
April 3, 2000

Ms. Eunice Alvarez
General Manager
Crystal Corporation
Boise, Idaho 83720

Dear Ms. Alvarez:

I am writing in response to your ad in Sunday's Inquirer for an assistant manager. I believe my experience is directly related to the position offered.

For the past five years, I have assisted the manager of XYZ Corporation. My duties have included drafting speeches, devising company manuals, and providing administrative support. Most recently, we worked together on a training manual for new employees. While I still find my present position challenging, I am seeking employment with greater growth potential.

Enclosed is a copy of my résumé. I look forward to hearing from you and meeting to discuss how my background applies to the assistant manager position at Crystal Corporation.

Sincerely,
Theresa Jobi

Each time you are going to write something, ask yourself: Do I know the reader? Picture in your mind the person or group you are addressing. If your picture is clear, you can focus your writing on that person's interests or needs. Consider your reader's relationship to you (relative, friend, colleague, teacher) and his or her familiarity with the subject. These considerations will affect the words you choose and the manner in which you express your thoughts.

Often, people have technical knowledge that they do not realize is technical. For example, accountants use certain terms so regularly that to them these terms seem commonplace. To the average person they are not.

Every specialty field—management information services, engineering, accounting, data processing, insurance, personnel—has its own language. People need to communicate clearly with clients and customers, as well as with other departments within their own organizations. When communicating with people not knowledgeable in your field, think about these suggestions:

- Recognize that you know a language that is not familiar to your audience.
- When explaining processes or procedures, include the extra step that you think is too obvious to state.
- When you must use a technical term, explain it briefly and clearly.
- Plan your writing so the nontechnical reader can follow it easily.
- When quoting necessary policy language, explain it in plain English.
- Determine which technical facts can be eliminated.

What Is Your Purpose?

Whether you are writing a letter to your congressperson or a book report for your teacher, you must have a clear purpose. Recognizing what you feel and think can be worlds apart from understanding the "purpose" of your writing. For example, you may feel angry that the dress you bought shrank when you washed it, but the purpose of your writing a letter to the store will be to persuade the owner to give you your money back. First, consider your basic motivation in writing. Are you going to berate your senator for voting against the Clean Air Bill, or will you congratulate him? Will your term paper support the idea that Hamlet had a tragic flaw, or will it show him as a victim of circumstance? Before you write, you must know what you want to say and why.

We're not used to thinking about why we're writing each time we pick up a pen or pencil. Yet everything we write does have a purpose. Our everyday communications are no exception. They have purposes, too:

- to inform
- to request
- to persuade
- to motivate
- to entertain

As the above list indicates, we may want to give or receive information (we *inform or request*), convince someone to believe the way we do (we *persuade*), or encourage someone to take action (we *motivate*). On occasion, we want our reader to laugh (we *entertain*). Almost all writing falls under the broad purposes of informing, requesting, persuading, motivating, or entertaining.

Our *business communications* must have clearly stated purposes:

- the memo to all department employees—to request notice of vacation dates.
- the letter to your client—to inform him that his claim has been denied.
- the report to your supervisor—to persuade her that the facts you give favor purchasing a new computer and to motivate her to order it immediately.

Our *more personal business communications* have clear purposes, too:

- the letter to an auto dealer—to inform the management about how poorly the car has worked since it was serviced and to motivate them to do something about it.
- the letter to fellow members of your labor union—to persuade them to vote for the political candidate who supports higher wages and better working conditions.
- the memo to the college registrar—to request a refund for the course you withdrew from last semester.

Our *everyday communications* also have purposes:

- the shopping list—to inform or remind us of what we need to buy.
- the note to the doctor's receptionist—to request insurance forms and to ask where to send those forms.
- the personal note on your holiday card to your letter carrier—to thank him or her for special service.
- the note to a family member—to persuade him or her to make a dental appointment.

PRACTICE 1

For each of the following situations, identify one or more purposes: to inform, to request, to persuade, to motivate, or to entertain. For example, consider a letter to a department store giving your new address. What is its purpose? To inform. Remember, too, that some of the examples are likely to have more than one purpose.

1. A memo to company team members reminding them of a project due date.
   Purpose: _____
   _____

2. A letter to a client regarding his overdue bill.
   Purpose: _____
   _____

3. A letter to your representative asking her not to vote for the budget increase.
   Purpose: _____
   _____

4. A newspaper ad featuring your company's product.
   Purpose: _____
   _____

5. An essay on your leadership ability, written for a college application.
   Purpose: _____
   _____

6. A memo to your boss stating the time and place of the monthly board meeting.
   Purpose: _____
   _____

7. A report listing all the products sold by a competing company, plus your conclusion to increase your company's product line.
   Purpose: _____
   _____

8. A term paper explaining the techniques an author used to create a character.
   Purpose: _____
   _____

9. A memo to the office staff, assigning regular parking spaces.
   Purpose: _____
   _____

10. A letter explaining to a utility company why you haven't paid your bill.
   Purpose: _____

   _____

Why Do You Need a Purpose?

Like most writers, you want to do more than just write a better memo, letter, or report; you want to get the writing done faster and less painfully. You can speed the process along if you decide on your purpose before you begin to write. Think about what you want the letter or memo to achieve. Establishing your purpose ahead of time will help you keep your thoughts centered on the writing task.

Remember your teachers' exams or essay questions? These gave you a purpose for writing.

Question: In his *Origin of Species,* Darwin used the term "natural selection." What did he mean?
Your purpose: To *inform* the reader of the definition of "natural selection" and give examples of it.

When you were in school, the questions you were asked served as clues to your writing purpose. Now you have to determine the purpose for yourself. And you have to put that purpose on paper and keep it in front of you as you write. Whenever you are stuck, your thoughts are wandering, or you are losing confidence, reread your purpose and move ahead.

You may be wondering how to write a purpose statement. Follow this simple formula or write your own:

My purpose for writing this _____ (memo, letter, report, essay, etc.) to _____ (name your reader) is to _____ (inform, request, persuade, motivate, entertain), so that my reader will _____ (name the action you want the reader to take or the information or belief you want him or her to have).

For example:

My purpose for writing this memo to the new supervisor is to inform her about the content of the company's safety training sessions so that she will be ready to handle her first meeting independently.

or:

My purpose for writing this letter is to persuade my appliance customers that our new service department can handle any repairs their appliances may need so that my customers will call us before they call another repairman.

When you know *why* you are writing something—your purpose—you are more likely to organize your thoughts effectively. For example, Daniel Martinez wants a job with the Edgemont Computer Corporation. Of course, he wants the company to know about his past sales record and his awards, so they will hire him. At this point, however, Dan wants the personnel director to see that his sales experience qualifies him for the advertised job. That's his purpose for writing the letter. If he accomplishes his purpose, Dan will probably get the interview he's asked for.

January 12, 2000

Ms. Gail Watson
Personnel Director
Edgemont Computer Corporation
979 6th Avenue
San Diego, California 92110

Dear Ms. Watson:

My sales experiences, detailed below, match the qualifications stated in your January 10 advertisement for a sales manager.

Four years ago, I began selling computers for Fairchild Computer Company. Within two years, I opened markets in all areas of the United States. After my promotion to sales manager in 1999, my duties required me to assemble a sales team, staff new sales offices in six major cities, and track the performance of our new sales force. Other details of my education and work experience are listed on the enclosed résumé.

I will be in San Diego the week of February 10 and would be able to meet with you any time then to answer any questions and discuss in greater detail how I could contribute to an increase in Edgemont Computer Corporation's sales. I will call early next week to see if we can set up an appointment.

Thank you for your consideration.

Sincerely,
Daniel Martinez

Memos, too, require a strong sense of purpose. In just a few lines, a memo must inform, request, persuade, or motivate.

MEMORANDUM

TO: Samuel Chang
FROM: Ed Felder
DATE: 2/6/00
SUBJECT: Annual Reference Book Order

Please add the books on the attached list to your library order. Thanks.

This was a memo to inform. Notice how the memo changes when the purpose changes:

MEMORANDUM

TO: Samuel Chang
FROM: Ed Felder
DATE: 2/6/00
SUBJECT: Request for decision on annual reference book order

The deadline for placing the book order is February 20. Since we missed out on the early order discount last year, let's try to make up the list earlier this year. I'll approve your booklist without delay, but only if I receive it within the next week.

In this second memo, the purpose—to request and encourage Samuel Chang to submit the necessary list on time—is hinted at through persuasion. There will not be delays if he gets it to Ed Felder on time. Ed's purpose is there, though it is not directly stated.

A more effective memo states the purpose more directly:

MEMORANDUM

TO: Samuel Chang
FROM: Ed Felder
DATE: 2/6/00
SUBJECT: Deadline for Early Order Discount

The deadline for placing the annual reference book order and receiving the discount is February 20. We missed out on the early order discount last year. Please submit your booklist within the week so your department can realize the savings. If I receive your recommendations later than February 13, I cannot guarantee processing in time to meet the 20th deadline.

The above example states the purpose, the deadline for early order discount, in the subject line, connects early order with department savings, and clearly states the impossibility of realizing the discount without timely information.

A letter, too, requires a clear purpose. Since business people do not have time to search through one or more pages of correspondence to ferret out the purpose, it should be stated early in the opening paragraph. You weaken your memo or letter by starting with the sentence "The purpose of this letter (memo) is…." You can clearly state your purpose by beginning:

I am writing to inform you that your insurance policy has expired.

This letter affirms our discussion to replace all 1998 trucks with 2001 models.

Please review the enclosed agreement and return two signed copies.

Macrocorporation will no longer purchase plastic replacement parts.

Reports for school seem to have the obvious purpose of telling a teacher that you've read the book or done the necessary research. Beyond that, however, your report has the purpose of informing the reader of the facts you have uncovered or the observations you have made about the book you read. Many times you will not be answering a question the teacher has posed; rather, you'll be formulating your own theory or idea, based on the purpose of informing the reader. For example, after having read Fitzgerald's *The Great Gatsby*, you have concluded that the book is not about Jay Gatsby so much as it is about Nick, the narrator. Your purpose is to persuade the reader that this is true, while also informing your teacher that you've read the book as assigned. Your report is likely to begin something like this:

In F. Scott Fitzgerald's novel *The Great Gatsby,* the narrator Nick Carraway is the focal point of the book. His journey from innocence to worldliness, through his acquaintances with Jay Gatsby, Daisy and Tom Buchanan, Jordan Baker, and the other characters, makes this novel a story of a young man growing up in a wasteland world...

Where Do You State Your Purpose?

In the example just given, the writer stated his main idea in the beginning paragraph. If we had included the rest of the report, you would see that he uses examples to prove the point that he states at the beginning. The reader knows what is being discussed, and the writing is clear and makes the point, whether the reader agrees or not.

PRACTICE 2

Read the following opening sentences of paragraphs from letters, memos, and reports. Is each purpose clearly stated? Is it to inform, request, persuade, or motivate? Write your answers in the space provided.

1. (Report)   Although there are still misinformed people who insist that alcoholism is caused by lack of willpower, scientific research shows that alcoholism is a disease.

    Purpose: _____

    _____

2. (Memo)   Please send me your department's sales figures for inclusion in the year-end report to the Board of Directors.

    Purpose: _____

3. (Letter)   I bought the washing machine marked "Large-Capacity, No. A-123," which you advertised would accommodate the clothes of a very large family; it doesn't. Please arrange for pickup and a refund.

    Purpose: _____

    _____

4. (Report)   Science fantasy, a subcategory of science fiction, bases its stories on natural laws of science, which are different from those we know to be true.

    Purpose: _____

    _____

5. (Letter)   We are looking for an investor who understands our industry's technology.

    Purpose: _____

    _____

PRACTICE 3

For each letter, memo, or report described in this exercise, write a purpose statement. To review writing a purpose statement, look back to page 6 and follow the instructions. Then, keeping your purpose in mind, write the letter, memo, or report as directed.

1. Write a business letter to Ms. Monica Viti at Consolidated Savings Bank. Request the bank's patience on your overdue auto loan. Discuss why you're asking for an extension, and explain how and when you'll make the payment. Include your address and the date. (See page 2.)

    Purpose: _____

    _____

2. Write a memo to Jim Hardy, Personnel Director. Ask him to look into the company's rising absentee rate and determine its causes. Include the *To, From, Date,* and *Subject* lines. (See page 8.)

    Purpose: _____

    _____

3. Write a one-paragraph introduction for a report entitled "Threats to Our Water Supply" for your local environmental group.

    Purpose: _____

    _____

4. Write a one-paragraph announcement to your customers stating that you are now the exclusive agents for Alphabeta Computers.

    Purpose: _____

    _____

5. Write a memo to your staff. Request that they submit a weekly sales summary instead of the usual monthly one. Include the *To, From, Date,* and *Subject* lines. (See page 8.)

    Purpose: _____

    _____

How Do I Say It Best?

Writing takes many forms: letters, memos, reports, notes, lists, and books, to name just a few. Depending on your intention, the form you choose will determine the structure of your writing. We discuss the forms of writing in greater detail in Chapter 4.

Formal and Informal Writing

We have discussed some basic questions you should ask yourself before you begin writing. If you have been thinking about who your reader is, then you've moved along to another fundamental aspect of writing: the levels of language. Usually we don't think much about language levels because most of the time we automatically choose the correct level for our purpose. Language, however, can be either formal or informal, depending on the choice of words, the arrangement of sentences, and the overall tone and structure. Both levels are correct when used at the appropriate times, but you should recognize the differences and know when to use each.

Writing to a friend, you would never say,

> Dear Thomas Grey:
>   Thank you for your note of June 18, 2000, inquiring about my health. The flu has passed and I have returned to work. . . .

Too formal! However, you might say,

> Dear Tom,
>   Thanks for your note. Yes, I had a terrible two weeks battling the flu, but I'm back at work now and feeling fine. . . .

What are the differences between these two letters? What makes one formal and the other informal? Think about the words each writer chose, the tone of the note, the feeling or frame of mind of each writer. Write your opinion on a sheet of paper and then compare it to the answer key at the end of the chapter.

More About Levels of Writing

If you were writing a letter to a prospective employer, you would *not* say:

> It was really great hearing from you. Sure, I'll come in for my second interview on December 2, 2000. I'll see you at about 9:00 A.M. Thanks again. . .

If you were serious about getting that job, you would write in a more formal style:

> Thank you for scheduling a second interview. I look forward to seeing you on December 2, 2000 at 9:00 A.M. . .

"Formal," however, does not mean stilted. Avoid words and phrases that are stiff and pompous, making you seem like a stuffed shirt. How would you react to this letter, and what impression would it leave?

> May I express my deep gratitude on having received your request for a second interview. You certainly can rely upon my arrival at your office promptly at 9:00 A.M.

Each time you write or speak, you choose—consciously or unconsciously—the level of language you want. You did not have to read this book to know that the first version—the informal one—sounds wrong considering the occasion and the reader. Being informal, however, does not always mean being incorrect. Used at the right time, an informal approach allows you to communicate in a more conversational tone, perhaps getting your idea across in a friendly, effective way. The conversational tone may be extremely light, as in the letter to Tom, or less so, as in this book.

Unless you are always engaged in casual correspondence with friends and relatives, you will need to raise the level of your communications. When you write business letters, memos, reports, and even letters or notes to acquaintances, you should avoid certain inappropriate words, phrases, and spellings. Instead:

1. Spell words as they were intended; for example, do not use *Xmas.* While it is used commercially, it is not appropriate in your writing. The same is true for *nite,* instead of *night, thru* instead of *through, pleez* instead of *please,* and *tho* instead of *though.*

2. Avoid slang, colloquialisms, or casual vocabulary and phrases associated with conversation. Examples: "Hey, buddy. Long time no see!" or "After our office received the new system, we were told to prepare for a shakedown cruise." Again, we are not suggesting that casual or informal is wrong; you just need to know where and when to use that vocabulary.

3. Avoid contractions of words. "*I'll* call the meeting to order at 2 P.M. sharp. Please be sure *you're* there on time." Although contractions have become more and more acceptable in informal writing, you need to decide whether or not they lower the level of your writing.

Which of the following three notes might the president of a major corporation write to one of his salesmen whose wife had just given birth to a boy?

Dear John:
    Congratulations to you and Maria on the birth of John, Jr. I know you will have many proud and happy years ahead.

                                        Sincerely,
                                        William Rivera

Dear John,
    Way to go! My best to you and Maria. There will be many times in the years to come when you and I will be raising our mugs for John, Jr.

                                        Best wishes,
                                        Bill

Dear Mr. Stillman:

I wish to extend my heartfelt congratulations to you and Mrs. Stillman on the birth of your son, John, Jr. I look forward to sharing your pride on future occasions.

Sincerely,
William Rivera

The first is the best for this situation; it is formal, but friendly. The second is unquestionably too informal; it would more likely be sent to a very close friend. The third choice is stilted and inappropriate when the reader and writer know each other well.

PRACTICE 4

Find and correct the words and phrases that are inappropriate for the occasions.

I.   MEMO
     To: Staff
     From: R. G. Ganz
     Subject: Manual

I hope you will all do the rite thing and finish your portions of the manual this month. We can work thru lunch each day if you want to.

II. MEMO
     Attn: Accounts Payable

Altho we've asked you not to, you're still sending our office two copies of every invoice.

III. Note to your teacher

     Hey, I know you asked for the term paper by Fri., but I won't be in school.

PRACTICE 5

When do you write in a formal tone? When would informal language be more suitable? You make the decision.

Listed below are occasions. Rate each occasion **F** for Formal or **I** for Informal.

	Occasion	*Formal or Informal?*
1.	A cover letter for your résumé.	_____
2.	A toast to your good friend on his 50th birthday.	_____
3.	A letter to your lawyer about a suit for damages.	_____
4.	A thank-you note to your grandmother.	_____
5.	A research paper for your psychology class.	_____

PRACTICE 6

Look at these statements from memos, letters, and reports. Are they too formal, too casual, or right for the occasion?

A.   MEMO

Well guys, here I am again, begging for your first quarter time sheets. Make this CEO happy and get 'em in this year!

Too Formal _____   Too Casual _____   Right for the Occasion _____

B.   Dear Miguel,

Where've you been, pal? You'd think my best friend would've congratulated me on my marriage!

Too Formal _____   Too Casual _____   Right for the Occasion _____

C.   The steady increase in phone calls resulting from our new website confirms our company's vision regarding the impact of the Internet. Therefore, at our next board meeting, where this report will be submitted for approval, we will request a significant increase in our on-line advertising budget.

Too Formal _____   Too Casual _____   Right for the Occasion _____

D.   Dear Ms. Johnson:

We are sorry about the confusion with your order. Our order department obviously recorded the wrong delivery date on your invoice. We have corrected the error and will deliver the furniture on the 18th as promised.

Your loyalty is important to us, and we would like to recognize that. Please visit the store again so that we can give you a discount coupon for any future purchase.

Too Formal _____   Too Casual _____   Right for the Occasion _____

E.   Dear Mrs. La Costa,

We're sorry Dan's passed on. He was one great guy. We'll miss him at the weekly game.

Too Formal _____   Too Casual _____   Right for the Occasion _____

PRACTICE 7

Think about the occasions on which you have had to write letters, memos, or reports for school, work, or personal reasons. Did you need to be formal or informal? Choose at least three of your experiences and describe them. Write a short description, similar to the ones you read in **PRACTICE 5**, page 15, for each of your examples. Rate each occasion **F** for Formal or **I** for Informal.

	Occasion	*Formal or Informal?*
1.		
2.		
3.		
4.		
5.		

Informal, Not Substandard

An informal level of writing is not the same as a substandard level. Substandard English includes faulty grammar, awkward sentence structure, and incorrect word usage. It is incorrect, no matter who the reader or listener. For example, it is unacceptable to say, "My foreman *don't* ever give me credit for good work," even if you're writing to your mother. Always follow the rules of standard written English.

PRACTICE 8

Test your understanding of the differences between informal and substandard language. As you read each sentence, decide whether it contains informal or substandard (incorrect) language. Check the appropriate column.

1. Here's the user manual you asked for.

   _____ Informal   _____ Incorrect

2. Our department hardly never takes time for lunch.

   _____ Informal   _____ Incorrect

3. Neither Smith nor Ono are ready to report.

   _____ Informal   _____ Incorrect

4. It's never too early for a coffee break.

   _____ Informal   _____ Incorrect

5. Glancing down the darkened street.

   _____ Informal   _____ Incorrect

As you proceed through this book, you will learn how to avoid the errors you found in **PRACTICE 8**. In the answer key, you will find the correct answers and the numbers of the chapters in which these errors are addressed.

Special Language

One of the first questions discussed in this book was "Who is your audience?" We mentioned that identifying your reader will help you set the tone of your writing. You should also ask yourself what your reader already knows about the subject in question. What information does he or she bring to the material? This is a critical question, especially when you are writing technical material. Don't risk annoying your reader by making him or her work too hard or, conversely, by oversimplifying. Use language that is appropriate to your reader's level of understanding.

Sometimes the simple addition of a few words will make the sentence clearer. Suppose you had to explain the forms of computer documentation. You might write this:

TUT-DOCs include one or more tasks for the user to perform.

Your reader may understand this if he or she is familiar with computer documentation. If your reader is not, the addition of four words clarifies the sentence:

TUT-DOCs are tutorial statements, lessons that include one or more tasks for the user to perform.

How effective do you think the following memo is in conveying the important information?

TO: All New Employees
FROM: Director of Employee Benefits

Please have all appropriate information regarding your EBP in my office before the payroll due date of this month. This should include FWT, BCBS, and MM data.

To all new employees? Do they know the payroll due date? Are they familiar with all of the abbreviations? Do they know what the appropriate information is? The writer of this memo would have saved time and subsequent explanatory phone conversations if he took more time to write a clearer memo:

TO: All New Employees
FROM: Director of Employee Benefits

Please have the following information regarding your Employee Benefits Program in my office by March 20, 2000, the payroll due date of this month:

        Name

        Address

        Social Security number

        Previous insurance policy number and carrier

        Number of dependents

        Names, ages, and birthdates of other members of your family to be included in insurance coverage.

This information is required for either federal withholding tax, Blue Cross/Blue Shield, or major medical insurance coverage.

PRACTICE 9

Decide whether each writing sample that follows is too formal, too informal, or just right for the occasion or purpose. Rewrite those that are not suitable.

1.   A father's note:

Dear David,

   As we agreed in our conversation of May 2, 2001, you will begin cleaning your room no later than May 3, 2001. Please schedule your homework and other activities accordingly.

                                               Very truly yours,
                                               Dad

2.   A business report:

Statement of Purpose:

   This is a proposal to provide the XYZ Corporation with a system for training department heads in effective written communication.

3.   A memo:

July 8, 2000
TO: All the Guys
FROM: Al
SUBJECT: Memos

You gotta stop writing so many memos.

4.   A résumé statement:

The ability to work with people—For a while now, I've worked with some guys in surveying.

5.   A term paper on computers, written for a teacher of computer education:

What is an 8-bit microcomputer? The term *8-bit* describes the microprocessor inside the microcomputer. The microprocessor is a semiconductor integrated circuit that is the heart of any microcomputer system.

ANSWERS

PRACTICE 1

1.   To inform.
2.   To inform.
3.   There are several purposes:
     a.   to *inform* your representative of the facts.
     b.   to *persuade* her that the facts require a "no" vote.
     c.   to *motivate* her to vote against the increase.
4.   There are several purposes:
     a.   to *inform* the reader about your product (price, size, functions, benefits).
     b.   to *persuade* the consumer that your product is the one to buy (it is less expensive, more efficient, stores conveniently).
     c.   to *motivate* the consumer to buy your product.
5.   There are several purposes:
     a.   to *inform* the reader with examples of your leadership ability.
     b.   to *persuade* the reader that you are the kind of student the college would want to accept.
     c.   to *motivate* the reader to accept you to the college.
6.   To inform.
7.   There are several purposes:
     a.   to *inform* by listing all the products.
     b.   to *persuade* management that increasing your company's product line is the right action to take.
     c.   to *motivate* management to act on your conclusion.
8.   To inform.
9.   To inform.
10. There are two purposes:
     a.   to *inform* the company about your special problems.
     b.   to *persuade* the company that the reasons you've given should prevent them from turning off service.

PRACTICE 2

All purposes are clearly stated.
1.   There are two purposes:
     a.   to *inform*, giving results of scientific research.
     b.   to *persuade* the reader to accept that alcoholism is a disease.
2.   To request.
3.   There are two purposes:
     a.   to *inform* the retailer what item the customer bought and that the purchase of this item was based upon the store's inaccurate advertisement.
     b.   to *request* that the washing machine be picked up.
4.   To inform the reader that one type of science fiction, science fantasy, does not base its stories on the laws of science as we know them.
5.   To inform the reader that the writer is interested only in an investor who understands a particular industry's technology.

PRACTICE 3
(Answers will vary.)

1. Purpose: To inform and persuade

   1 Primrose Lane
   Warwick, Rhode Island 02888
   May 15, 2001

   Ms. Monica Viti
   Loan Manager
   Consolidated Savings Bank
   123 Main Street
   Boston, MA 02864

   Dear Ms. Viti:

   You have every reason to expect prompt payment on auto loans. I regret that I have been unable to send a payment this month. I am relying on your patience and my previously perfect payment record to get us through this difficult time.

   For the past six months, I have been unemployed. For five of those months, I have managed to pay all my bills. However, by this past month my savings were exhausted.

   Fortunately, I have just been rehired by my company. In order to meet all my obligations, though, I will have to send partial back payments to my creditors.

   As of June 1, I will resume my auto loan payment. In addition, I will add 20% of the past-due amount. In this way, my account will be current in five months. Thank you for your patience and cooperation.

   Sincerely,

2. Purpose: To inform and to request information

   TO: Jim Hardy, Personnel Director
   FROM: Andrea Vargas
   DATE: December 19, 2000
   SUBJECT: Rising Absentee Rates

   I have noticed in the past three months that our absentee rate has risen from 2.8 to 3.6 percent (using the Bureau of Labor Statistics formula). The absences are surprising since a recent survey revealed that employees are generally content with both the working conditions and the new pay scale.

   Please take the following first steps to find out why absenteeism has increased.

   1. Find out who—if any—are the chronic absentees.
   2. Find out whether the absentee rate is higher in certain departments than in others.

   Let's meet on February 2 to discuss what you've learned.

3. Purpose: To inform and motivate

   We need water for life, yet most people take it for granted. We expect to turn on a faucet and get good-quality water because in the United States water has always been plentiful, clean, and cheap. However, too little rain in certain areas, an increased demand for water in all areas, and the new threat of pollution from toxic waste disposal make future supplies uncertain.

4. Purpose: To inform and persuade

Dear Customer:

We know you have been waiting for this good news! We are now the exclusive New England sales agent for the XYZ Computer Company. We'll be able to offer you the latest Alphabeta Computer—the one so many of our customers have wanted. Of course, we will also stock the software and handle any servicing problems that occur.

5. Purpose: To inform

TO: Staff
FROM: June D. Levine
DATE: 12/1/00
SUBJECT: Change to weekly sales summaries

As of January 1, 2001, please submit a weekly sales summary instead of the usual monthly one. Thanks.

FORMAL AND INFORMAL WRITING

Answers may vary, but you should note that the language used in the first letter on page 12 is what makes that letter more formal: the person addressed using both first and last names, and the formal reference to "your note of June 18, 2000," whereas in more casual writing the date would not be mentioned. The phrase "inquiring about my health" is stiff and unfriendly.

In the second letter, the phrase "thanks . . . note" is friendly and has a light tone; the phrase "yes…fine" is conversational, as if the writer and reader were face to face.

PRACTICE 4

I. MEMO
    To: Staff
    From: R. G. Ganz
    Subject: Manual

I hope you will all do the right *thing* and finish your portions of the manual this month. We can work *through* lunch each day if you want to.

II. MEMO
    Attn: Accounts Payable

Although we have asked you not to, *you are* still sending our office two copies of every invoice.

III. Note to your teacher

I know you asked for the term paper by *Friday*, but I will not be in school.

PRACTICE 5
1. F
2. I
3. F
4. I
5. F

PRACTICE 6
A. Too casual
B. Right for the occasion
C. Right for the occasion
D. Right for the occasion
E. Too casual

PRACTICE 7
(Answers will vary. The following are sample answers.)

	Occasion	Formal/Informal
1.	cover letter for a résumé	formal
2.	letter to colleagues requesting a meeting	informal
3.	letter of recommendation for a friend	formal
4.	letter requesting that a store correct your account balance	formal
5.	memo to your new boss requesting a parking space	formal

PRACTICE 8
1. Informal
2. Incorrect (Our department hardly *ever* takes time for lunch.) See Chapter 8.
3. Incorrect (Neither Smith nor Ono *is* ready to report.) See Chapter 7.
4. Informal
5. Incorrect (glancing down the darkened street) See Chapter 7.

PRACTICE 9
1. This is too formal for the occasion. Here is a less formal version:

    Dear David,

    Yesterday we talked about when you would clean your room. You said that you would do it today between baseball and study time. Please do.

    Love,
Dad

2. Just right for the purpose.
3. Too informal for the purpose. The memo sounds as if the message could be spoken rather than written. "Gotta" is incorrect English.
4. Too informal for the purpose. Here is a more suitable statement: Since 2000, I have worked on several land surveying teams.
5. Just right for the purpose.

2.

Save Time by Planning

None of us likes to waste time with preliminaries. We are eager to get words down on paper and see something tangible. For the fortunate few, forging ahead without a plan may work; but most of us need to develop some type of plan for our writing. The old adages, "A stitch in time saves nine" and "Haste makes waste," developed because of real-life experiences. They apply to writing, too.

Preliminary Preparation

Some of us can work only when surrounded by our favorite clutter; others can work only at an absolutely clean desk. Your preferred style of working is not important; preparing for it is. If you are the clean-desk type and must begin a task at 8 A.M., make certain that your desk is in order the day before.

Details that may seem unrelated to writing can cause delays if you haven't attended to them earlier. Do you have enough paper on hand? Is memory available in your computer? Will you need a calculator? Is the light sufficient?

Another aspect of planning is to let people know that you have a task with a deadline. If you can, request no phone calls or interruptions while you are preparing your report or special letter. If not, at least try to clear short blocks of uninterrupted time.

Planning includes thinking, talking, and jotting down notes. We plan to write long before we actually sit down with pen and pad, typewriter, or word processor. When do you get your most creative thoughts? Chances are that they do not come when you are fighting a deadline and consciously, perhaps frantically, trying to write.

Most people get creative thoughts when their minds are relaxed. That means when they are driving or sitting on a train or a bus, taking a shower, falling asleep, relaxing in the yard or on the beach. How does this translate into writing? Carry a small notebook. Jot down thoughts and insights related to writing projects when they occur. Unless you record them, you will not necessarily remember them tomorrow, or even in an hour.

If you have a major report or writing project, label a file and throw in notes as you think of them. Your notes need not be well written. They don't even have to be complete sentences. This way, when you do finally sit down to write, you will have words to put on that blank paper.

Plan Your Writing

Planning is the first step to good writing.
Outlining is the logical second step—usually.
Writing a draft follows—usually.
Editing is next.
Rewriting is last.

We suggest that outlining is usually the next step after planning. Some people just will not outline first. They plunge right into the first draft as a form of "mental dump." If that is your style and it works for you, do it. However, your next step must then be to outline. At some stage early in the writing process, you must organize your thoughts. Later in this chapter you will learn how to do this, but planning also includes some earlier considerations.

First you must have the necessary information and tools available. For example, when you get to the budget page of the proposal, you don't then start calling Payroll to verify the amounts.

Consider these aspects of planning:

1. What facts or figures do you need to write that report, proposal, letter, or memo? Compile these data before you start to write.
2. Did you write a similar report or proposal last year? Did someone else? Use it as a model if it was well received.
3. Have you previously written to or received letters from the person to whom you are now writing? Have all correspondence on hand for easy reference.
4. Are you planning enclosures with your letter? Make sure the enclosures are available when you need them.
5. Does the letter require scheduling or a follow-up phone call? Have a calendar available. You don't want to say you'll call on the 10th if that's a Sunday.
6. Do you have to schedule computer time? Do you need the copy machine? Book these in advance if their availability may be a problem.
7. Are you going to ask someone else to type your report on the computer? Don't assume that, if your report is due Thursday, you can hand it to her on Wednesday night and have it the next morning. She may have other plans.

Now that you have prepared for your writing, let's plan the actual writing.

Develop an Outline

One of the least favorite memories you may have from school, second only to diagramming sentences, is writing outlines. Usually things would go well as far as Roman numeral III, at which point you would have an A entry but couldn't come up with a B entry if your life depended on it. Once again, we are discussing writing and—guess what?—outlining still makes sense. Don't close the book yet. Let's think it through.

An outline is simply a plan, a way of organizing. By organizing your thoughts in an outline form, you can see clearly what direction your writing will take. The more detailed your outline, the easier your first draft will be because you will have the facts and ideas in the order in which you plan to present them.

Your outline will vary, of course, with the type of writing you are doing. You will have to tailor your outline to the task at hand. A much more structured, detailed outline is appropriate for a business report or proposal or term paper, while a brief, sketchy outline is adequate for a one-page business letter. But outlining a short letter is helpful, too. By deciding the major topics you wish to cover and assembling the supporting details for each topic, right off you clarify in your mind what you plan to say and reserve the job of rewriting to tighten and sharpen your first draft.

One reason many people avoid outlining is that outlining, as we all learned it, requires us to organize our thoughts. Usually, however, as we approach a writing project, our thoughts are not yet organized. What is Roman numeral I? What subtopics support I? What main points follow it? When we first sit down to write, we do not have all these answers. A less structured approach to outlining helps free our thoughts. There are a number of ways to free your thoughts, but, for the most part, they begin with brainstorming.

Brainstorming

Brainstorming is a skill that can be used very effectively by a group to generate ideas, or by an individual for essentially the same reason. What happens when writers brainstorm or free-associate when they need to write on a topic? They write down any ideas that come to mind—any and all ideas that occur to them. However, a few important rules apply to brainstorming. You must not criticize or evaluate what you are writing down. All ideas are possible. Nothing you write is judged or considered wrong. Many of your brainstorming results will appear in your finished piece of writing, but some may not. You will make that decision later, after you have had a chance to organize these initial thoughts. Remember: When you brainstorm, don't judge; just take a clean sheet of paper and write, scribble, or jot down your thoughts.

Some writers prefer to jot down the main idea or purpose in the center of a blank page, and then begin placing every thought that relates to that idea or purpose in a pinwheel formation. The freedom of this brainstorming exercise is that you can jot your ideas all over the paper (see Diagram 1). This, too, helps generate thought. Note that the writer finished the brainstorm exercise, reread it, and decided that one of the ideas did not belong in this particular report. That one idea has been crossed out.

Brainstorming Outline — Step I

The logical second step to brainstorming an outline is organizing your random ideas. You see that carried out in Diagram 2. The writer has organized her outpourings on the subject (changes in management styles during the past decade) by designating three of her ideas as the major ones to be covered in the report:

1. Greater tendency toward participatory management
2. Greater interest in workers' personal needs
3. Many companies reach out to workers' families

Each of those topics is supported by important details, and you see the details as offshoots in the diagram. For example, "Managers have learned that seeking staff input improves productivity" becomes a supporting detail for major topic number 1, above. Note, too, that an even greater level of detail appears in the two items that are offshoots of detail 1 above. To check your understanding of this process, write those two second-level details or offshoots here:

1.
2.

(Check your answer in the ANSWERS section at the end of the chapter.)

   Now that the major topics and supporting details have been identified, the writer can begin the draft. You will read more about that in Chapter 3.

Brainstorming a List

The brainstorming pinwheel is not the only way to get your ideas on paper. You can begin in the same way—brainstorming, freeing your mind to come up with great ideas—but then you may choose to record them differently. If all you can manage at this point is a list, then do that. Write the words and phrases of your thoughts in a list, *but do not attempt to organize them in this first step.* Remember that your mind does not always work linearly (in a step-by-step manner), and if you force yourself to think only in a straight line, you will waste time. So, plan on rearranging the major thoughts after you have written them.

As an example, think of the travel agent who wanted to write a letter in response to a prospective client's request for cruise information. The agent's original thoughts tumbled onto paper and became this list:

airport departure
ocean liner departure
luggage requirements
total fee
air fees
land fees
ship fees
recommended ports of call
lines that service the recommended ports of call

Brainstorming Exercise — Step II

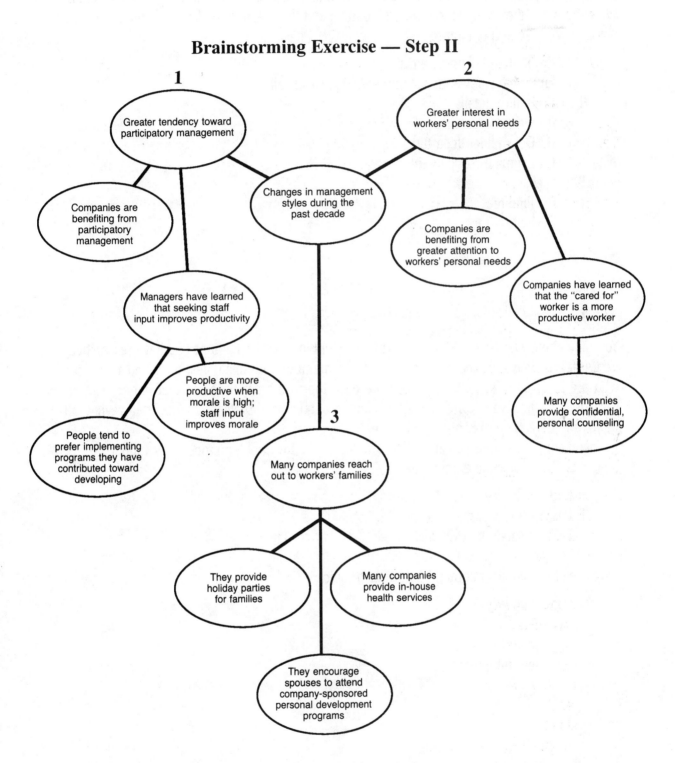

In what order do you think this agent eventually placed the major ideas? After putting the list aside for a while, he saw that, to entice the customer, the last two items should come first. He reorganized the items, grouping them into major categories of information, plus details. When he wrote the letter, he followed the outline and the writing took less time than if he had not brainstormed and organized first.

    I.   Recommended ports of call
   II.   Lines that service the recommended ports of call
  III.   Departure details
       A. Airport departure
       B. Ocean liner departure
       C. Luggage requirements
  IV.   Fees
       A. Total fee
       B. Itemized fees
          1. air
          2. land
          3. ship

The Topic Outline

You may already know what topics must be covered in a report. Perhaps you have researched, performed a brainstorming exercise with team members or colleagues, or talked to people who are involved in some way. If so, write each topic on a separate piece of paper or index card or input into your computer. Add relevant details in abbreviated form. Then review all topics and determine the appropriate order.

For example, assume you must write a report on the problems posed by modern office buildings. Your major topics might be

    Lack of privacy
    Lack of "fresh" air
    Difficult safety precautions

Here are some details that might follow each topic:

    Lack of privacy
      Causes
        no doors
        no soundproofing
        low walls

Effects
>   reluctance to speak confidentially on the phone or in person
>   frequent interruptions by those passing by or standing up to stretch
>   difficulty in concentrating

Lack of "fresh" air
>   Causes
>   windows do not open
>   fans are either absent or noisy
>   Effects
>   people become less energetic
>   productivity decreases

Difficult safety precautions
>   Causes
>   multistory buildings
>   possible power failures
>   windows that do not open
>   Effects
>   people may have to walk up or down 5 or more flights of stairs
>   people cannot readily access fresh air

You can see that the topics have led to significant details and, in effect, created an outline.

Subheadings

For reports, proposals, and even long letters and memorandums, include subheadings to make your writing reader-friendly. Subheadings also make your writing writer-friendly. They give you a clear course to follow.

For example, if you are writing a letter requesting approval to attend a conference, you might include these subheadings:

>   Purpose of Conference
>   Relevance to Current Challenges
>   Relevance to Future Needs
>   Conference Details

At this point, you may feel ready to write the letter, report, proposal, or memo, guided by the subheadings. Or you might want to brainstorm to gather the details before you begin writing. For example:

    I. Purpose of Conference
       A. Help secretaries and administrative assistants gain the management skills they need.
       B. Build the interpersonal skills that accompany success.
       C. Learn about:
          1. time management
          2. conflict resolution
          3. problem solving
   II. Relevance to Current Challenges
       A. Build a professional image.
       B. Gain control of projects through scheduling and planning.
       C. Master meeting planning.
  III. Relevance to Future Needs
       A. Understand the company's need to change.
       B. Understand the need for team building.
       C. Learn to facilitate team efforts.
  IV. Conference Details
       A. Date and time
       B. Place

Some Final Points About Outlining

Have we convinced you that you should use some form of an outline before you write? You have many options. If you decide to write a traditional or topic outline, follow these suggestions:

1. Decide on the major topics to be covered. The scope of these topics and the extent of your list will vary with the intent of your writing.
2. Review each major topic and determine the key supporting details for each.
3. Add any minor details for each key detail that you wish to include. Develop subgroupings as you need them.
4. Arrange the major topics as they best suit your purpose. Arrange the minor topics appropriately under each major topic.

Sometimes you will create a simple outline as this writer did in preparation for a memo to the company's team leaders. The main topic of the memo concerns learning to give and take helpful feedback during evaluations.

Team leaders should

    I. consider this an opportunity to build direct relationships with team members.
   II. work on taking (as well as giving) feedback positively.
  III. base evaluations on preset goals.
  IV. help team members learn to give feedback to others.

Other times, you may feel that you need to work from a more detailed outline. The following is an outline for a report on a company's need to address customer satisfaction.

    I.   Who are our customers?
        A. Focus on the right customers for our company.
        B. Who are the potential and former customers?
        C. What methods are we using to identify them?
    II.   How do we link improved customer service to an improved product?
        A. Involve customers.
        B. Involve management.
        C. Involve team members.
    III.   Who should be involved in addressing customer satisfaction?
        A. Develop a company-wide strategy.
        B. Understand that customer focus affects everyone from management to hourly workers.
        C. Understand that customer service emanates from leadership.
    IV.   Does service affect the bottom line?
        A. Evaluations we can do.
        B. Measures we can use.

For some people, identifying just the major topics is enough help in writing a letter. For reports and letters longer than a page or two, however, you will need to include more details in your outline, but these details will simplify the actual writing.

Remember, you are outlining for yourself. This is not a document on which you will be graded, nor will you attach it to your business report. Its purpose is to help you organize your thoughts. If it were for anyone other than yourself, you would want consistency—all complete sentences or all balanced phrases. Don't agonize over form or complete sentences. Get your thoughts into the structure. If the thought comes to you in a sentence, write it as a sentence. If it comes to you in a phrase or a word, write it as a phrase or a word.

The outline is not carved in stone, either. Once you complete it, review it. Is Roman numeral I really the first point you want to make? You can move entire sections of your outline around like pieces in a puzzle until they fit together in a way that seems best to you.

PRACTICE 1

Assume you are going to write on one of the following topics. Either brainstorm some ideas and jot them down in pinwheel fashion or in a list and then organize, or write a topic outline or subheadings.

1. A three-page paper discussing the effects of the Women's Movement on men, women, and marriage.
2. A letter to the president of an automobile corporation complaining about the many problems you have had with your car and the poor service you received from your dealer. Include a request for compensation.

PRACTICE 2

Select one of your brainstorm outlines and develop Step II.

PRACTICE 3

Assume you are going to write a letter to your boss, telling her how much you have enjoyed working for her and why you must leave for another position. Think about what you plan to say by making a list (then grouping), listing subtopics, or listing subheadings. Then develop an outline of key details under each subtopic or heading.

ANSWERS

Brainstorming Exercise Step II
(answer to question posed on page 28)

Second-level details:
1. People tend to prefer implementing programs they have contributed toward developing.
2. People are more productive when morale is high; staff input improves morale.

These are sample answers. Your answers will differ in content, but the style should be the same. We have provided examples of both the pinwheel diagram and a topic outline for the women's movement issue. For the automobile complaint, we have given only the diagram. You may continue with an outline.

PRACTICE 1, 2

1. The Effects of the Women's Movement on Men, Women, and Marriage

Brainstorming Exercise — Step I

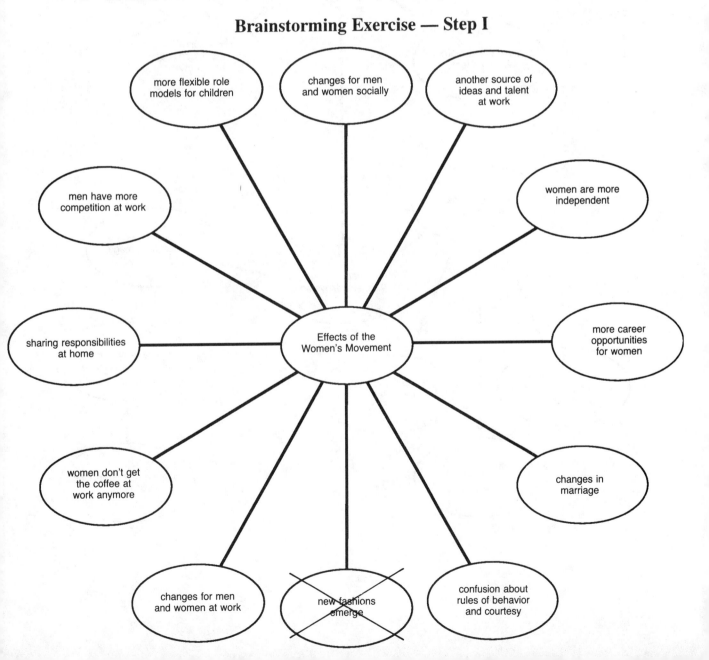

Brainstorming Outline — Step II

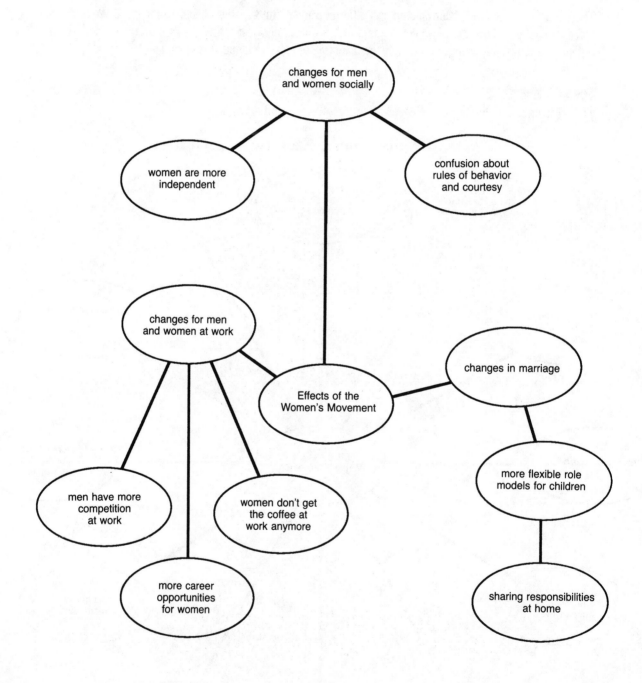

A.   Topic Outline
The effects of the women's movement:
Changes for men and women socially
Changes for men and women at work
Changes in marriage

B.   Topic Outline with Details
The effects of the women's movement:
    I. Changes for men and women socially
       A. Women are more independent
       B. Confusion about rules of behavior and courtesy
   II. Changes for men and women at work
       A. Men have more competition at work
       B. More career opportunities for women
       C. Women don't get the coffee at work anymore
  III. Changes in marriage
       A. More flexible role models for children
       B. Sharing responsibilities at home

2.   Letter of Complaint About Automobile Performance

Brainstorming Exercise — Step I

2. Letter of complaint about automobile performance.

Brainstorming Outline — Step II

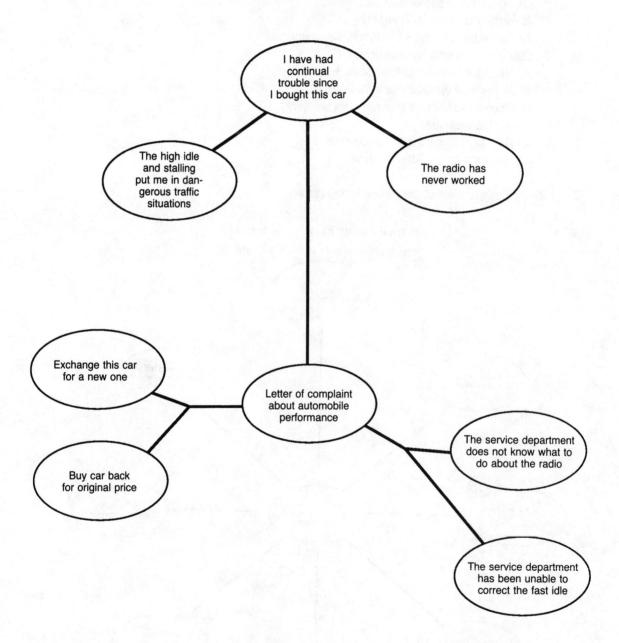

PRACTICE 3
This is a sample answer. Your answer will differ in content, but the style should be the same.

    I.   Enjoyed working there
        A. Freedom to implement ideas
        B. Consistent support and cooperation
   II.   No opportunity for advancement
        A. Salary and position have not increased
           1. Limited funding of nonprofit organization
           2. Agency policy against hiring from within
        B. Advancement is necessary for personal growth
  III.   Excellent opportunity available elsewhere
        A. Greater financial reward
        B. Faster career development
  IV.   Will remain in communication
        A. To assist successor
        B. To continue friendship

3.

Write Your First Draft

Even the most experienced writers write a first draft. The draft gives you the opportunity to get your words on paper while your creativity is flowing, without bogging you down with the details of form and structure. Write your first draft as quickly as possible. Follow your outline but flesh it out with sentences and paragraphs.

What If You Don't Outline First?

Okay, you tried. You wrote an outline but you hated every minute of it. You just don't work that way. You can't. You don't want to.

There is another approach, and it could work for you. Create first; revise later. Let's say you have to write a report for your boss. You have a lot of good ideas, but they are disorganized, and you don't know where to start. What do you do? Start anywhere. Just take a pen, pencil, or use your computer and begin writing down those thoughts. For example, write a list of ideas, as we suggested in Chapter 2. When you know that one idea absolutely should not follow the preceding one, leave a space. Continue to put those thoughts down on paper—any way they come to you. If you prefer, use index cards. They'll be easy to shuffle around later. The important thing is to start writing.

Now, an hour later, you have seven pages of unorganized notes. Fix yourself a cup of coffee, drink a can of soda, or go for a short walk. Take a break.

When you have had a chance to think about other things for a while, sit down again with your outpouring. You are not going to outline, but you are going to organize. Read through those notes. At some point, you will recognize a logical beginning for your report. Put a number 1 in the margin at that point. Locate the sentence or paragraph that logically follows 1 and number that 2. Continue in this fashion.

Type up those notes in the numbered order, leaving a lot of space between sentences and in the margins. You now have your outline, or plan, or beginning, or whatever you want to call it. This plan you have written will not necessarily be a symmetrical outline, with matching or parallel thoughts and balanced lists of evidence or examples. You may have a one-sentence paragraph and then a seven-sentence paragraph. Perhaps not all of your minor points will have the evidence necessary to support them. But you have written down and organized all your major thoughts; now you can more easily fill in the blanks. And now you are ready to write your first draft.

Full Speed Ahead!

With or without an outline, ploughing through a draft without pausing to sculpt the sentences may seem difficult at first. Do it anyway. You will have all of your ideas on paper, with half the battle over.

If you ever have taken a multiple-choice test, you'll remember that you were advised to answer all the easy questions first, then go back over those you skipped because they required more thought. The same is true of your first draft. Get the major ideas down on paper with as many supporting details as come readily.

Use markers to show the words or phrases that give you trouble. Markers are blanks, lines, or dots, and they will remind you to give special attention to those thoughts later. If you are typing the draft, double- or triple-space the lines. If you're writing it out in longhand, leave blank lines. This extra space will make editing and revising easier. If you don't have enough space on the page to make a change or improvement, you might just talk yourself out of making it.

Remember, when you are writing, two people are trying to get your attention—the writer and the editor. When the writer is writing, the editor should be locked out of the room. The writer should not slow down to seek the perfect word, correct the punctuation, check the verb tenses. The writer must keep writing to avoid losing the train of thought. The editor's job comes later.

Be Prepared to Make Changes

Many people get "married" to the first words they put on paper. Loyalty to these words will only lead to painful separations later. Realize that, although you might be very proud of your first draft, and it may be excellent, it is still a first draft. Most writing can be improved upon. If at all possible, wait a day or two before you edit or expand your draft. This lapse will give you a chance to become more objective, less committed to your first thoughts.

You say, "Who has the time for that?" But you have to include "simmering time" in your schedule even if you are a student with a term paper to write. Count on at least overnight, and preferably a day or two, to let thoughts settle. If you say, "I don't have the time," think again. The consequences of a poorly written memo, letter, or report can be severe or embarrassing. If you *really* don't have the time to allow the draft to "simmer," at least put off revising until after lunch or a coffee break. Don't go directly from creating to revising to sending or handing in your communication. Leave yourself time and space to think. If you have ever written and sent a letter and later felt your stomach drop as you reviewed your copy after "thinking time and space," you know the importance of distance.

Now Let's Write

If you followed the steps in Chapters 1 and 2, you focused on your purpose and developed an outline. The draft is the meat on the bones.

Suppose you must write a memo to another department head about the responsibilities your departments share. You have brainstormed and developed the following outline of your major issues. For example:

I. The functions of our departments are very similar.
    A. We answer product complaints.
    B. We build brand identification.
II. There is confusion as to clear division of duties, resulting in ineffective actions or lack of any action.
    A. Clients are sometimes placed in the middle of jurisdictional disputes.
    B. Clients are sometimes ignored, from lack of clear responsibility.
    C. Employees appear incompetent or uninformed.
III. Recommendations.
    A. Develop individual departmental goals.
    B. Hold joint meeting.
       1. Review departmental procedures.
       2. Set up procedures for referral.
       3. Establish a system of checks.

Your draft might begin as follows:

> The functions of departments A and X have always been interrelated. Both departments are designed to answer product complaints and build brand identification. Both departments have been staffed with workers dedicated to those purposes.
>
> In recent years, however, our related goals have crossed lines and led to some confusion. Because the separate functions of our departments are unclear, we sometimes approach the same client from two directions simultaneously. Too often lately, a client has not been served by either department. Ⓘam noticing a confusion and a _____ among my staff and assume you notice the same in your department.

Notice that the draft fills in tone and detail that the outline lacked. Occasionally, for lack of the right word, a blank or marker is used. Remember, this is a draft, not a final copy. The author did not like using the personal pronoun, *I*, and circled it as a reminder to rethink that sentence.

PRACTICE 1

Write the final paragraph for the above memo, following item III in the outline.

PRACTICE 2

Assume that your topic for a report is "Everyone Must Help Maintain Our Environment." Brainstorm the topic, using the pinwheel format. Place this statement in the center of your paper: The impact individuals have on the environment. Place all your thoughts on the pinwheel. Then decide which are main ideas and which are details. Finally, from the pinwheel, develop a topic outline.

PRACTICE 3

Now, use your brainstorm outline to write the first two paragraphs of the report.

PRACTICE 4

For practice, use the following statement as the first sentence in the final section of the report on the environment. See how quickly you can write a paragraph to support the topic sentence.

We can all recycle within our home environments.

For a clue, think about your garden, your old newspapers, your wire hangers, and so on.

PRACTICE 5

Write a rough draft for each of the following. Remember that your draft will flow more easily if you use one of the outline formats (pinwheel, topical, subtopics), then write an outline.

1. A letter to your child's teacher asking for better teacher-parent communication.
2. A memo to a coworker asking for help in writing a report with a tight deadline.
3. The first paragraph of an essay on any one of the following topics: (a) why cats make better pets than dogs; (b) the pros and cons of allowing employers to pay teenagers less than the minimum wage; (c) the appropriate minimum drinking age.

PRACTICE 6

The following notes for a letter were written by a person who chose not to outline. Applying the listing or numbering technique described earlier, arrange the information in a logical way. Then write the letter.

Dear Ms. Reyes:

Enjoyed meeting you at the convention. Innovative and exciting ideas. Eager to implement in our district. Presentation well planned and presented. Great deal of information. Need *Prospectus*. Please visit. Excellent workshop. Thanks for valuable presentation.

Sincerely,

ANSWERS

These are sample answers. Your answers will necessarily differ in content.

PRACTICE 1

To solve this problem before it reaches major proportions, I propose the following:

Each department should review the existing goals that have been set down for it and then break down those goals into individual staff operations. Let's also schedule a meeting in the near future for representatives from each department to review joint goals. At that meeting, the representatives can further clarify the differences in duties and/or exchange some duties if preferable. The representatives will bring the results of this meeting to their departments for additional review and possible revision. We can hold a final meeting to assess these reactions and finalize the breakdown of departmental operations.

PRACTICE 2

Topic Outline

The impact individuals have on the environment

Paper products
- Colored dyes pollute waterways when paper products dissolve in sewer water and this water empties into rivers and streams
- Buying only white paper products will help prevent this form of pollution

Solid waste
- Bottles, cans, and packaging that encases them—general disposal problem all communities have
- Establish and use a local recycling center

Toxic waste
- Companies dump toxic waste
- If one is in your community
  - Be aware of potential hazards to children/animals
  - Find out more about the company; keep current
  - Report flagrant violations to the proper authorities

PRACTICE 3

Few people realize the impact they, as individuals, have on the environment. Occasionally, when specific instances are called to our attention, we become aware of this connection with our environment, but we quickly and conveniently forget it again. For example, the colored dyes in paper products pollute our waterways when these paper items, such as toilet tissue, dissolve in sewer water and this water empties into rivers and streams. We can avoid this form of pollution by making a conscious effort to buy only white paper products.

Solid waste, such as bottles and cans and the packaging that encases them, adds to a general disposal problem all communities have to deal with. We can diminish the solid waste problem on an individual basis by avoiding disposable bottles and cans. If we must buy goods in aluminum cans, we can work to establish and use a local recycling center.

Many of us adversely affect the environment without realizing it in other ways, too, such as…or when we…

The topic sentence is followed by supporting details. The writer knows more examples are needed but is uncertain as to what they might be. By leaving blanks, the writer can continue with more productive writing and return to this trouble spot later.

Brainstorming Outline — Step I

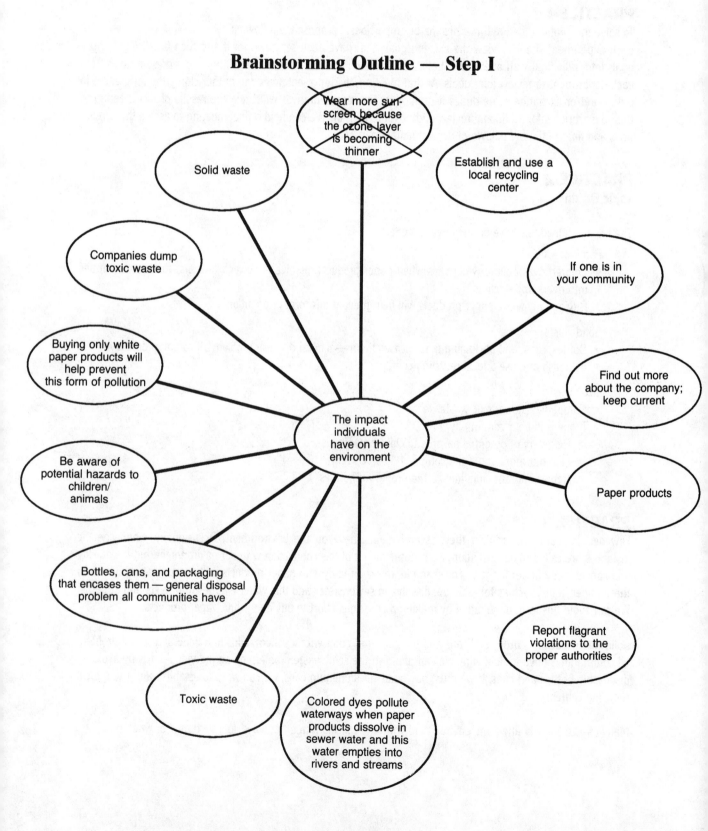

Brainstorming Outline — Step II

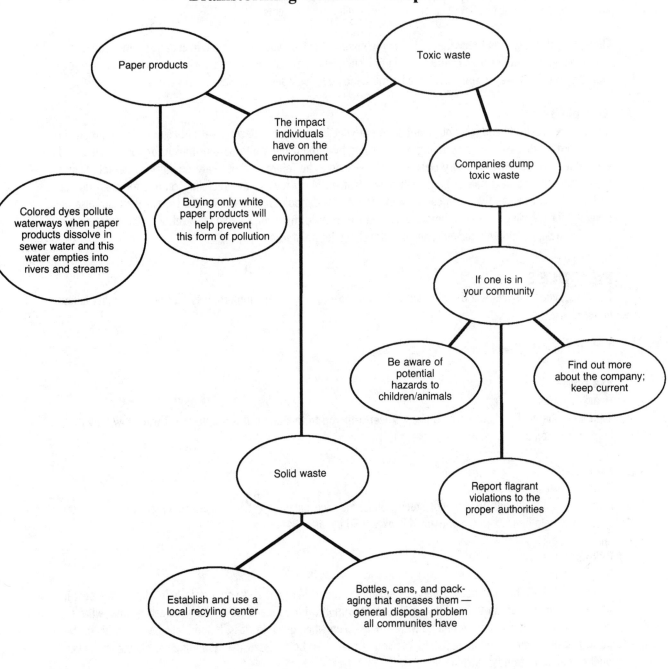

PRACTICE 4
Example A

We can all recycle within our home environments. If you have a garden in your backyard, you have an excellent spot to set up a compost bin, and can recycle kitchen refuse such as eggshells, coffee grounds, fruit and vegetable peels, and other organic leftovers. This compost pile will break down, and you'll soon have friable soil to use as fertilizer and mulch. Choose a spot near your garden and not far from your kitchen door. Then feed your compost pile daily with scraps, giving it a turn and a sprinkling of water and fresh soil every few days. Avoid adding any animal wastes, however, because those will attract rodents.

There is a lot to say about recycling in the home environment, so you might have included several suggestions in one paragraph, rather than concentrate on one suggestion, as did the writer above. If you chose to give several suggestions, however, you would need a more inclusive topic sentence. Here is an example:

Example B

If you think creatively enough, you might soon put your local refuse collection out of business. For example, in a backyard garden you can recycle organic leftovers by turning them into natural mulch for your flowers and vegetables. Furthermore, your dry cleaner would welcome the return of those wire hangers, to be able to use them again for the next pair of pants you have cleaned. Many towns have recycling centers for glass bottles and aluminum cans, and you can collect your empties for periodic trips to the center. Newspapers can also be collected for recycling in a neighborhood, or you can recycle them on a personal level by using them as gift wrap, for making children's cut-outs, and as drop cloths for painting.

PRACTICE 5

Of course, your answers will differ in content from those given. What's important is that your thoughts follow logically.

1. Letter to a child's teacher

Example 1
Dear Ms. Torres:
Todd is not happy in school. I would like to meet with you to talk about this problem so I will know how I can help him at home.

Example 2
Dear Ms. Torres:
I am very unhappy with Todd's poor study habits. May we please meet to discuss how you and I can work together to help him? I can see you any day except Friday after 3.

Example 3
Dear Ms. Torres:
I realize that Todd has not been a very responsible student. My goal and yours is to help him do his best in school. I think we can do this by staying in close communication. Please let me know ahead of time what his assignments will be, making certain he writes them down when given in class. If Todd falls behind in his homework, please let me know immediately. I've found that once he's missed five assignments, he becomes overwhelmed and has trouble catching up.

2. Memo to a coworker

Example 1
TO: John Barry
FROM: Maria Santiago
SUBJECT: Monthly Production Report
I just learned that I am now responsible for this report, which is due next week. Since you do such reports regularly, could we please meet as soon as possible so I can ask you some questions and establish a form?

Example 2
TO: Farouk Gandhi
FROM: Bill Martin
SUBJECT: Monthly Report
I am now working on our department's monthly report. Your recent research will be the major focus, and I would appreciate your assistance in organizing the necessary information. Unfortunately, I must complete the report by Wednesday. Please call by tomorrow so we can set a time to meet.

3. Essay paragraph

Example A
Why cats make better pets than dogs

Cats have a quiet dignity that dogs lack, making them better pets. When a cat wants attention, it will rub against you, nuzzle you, gently place a paw on you, and purr like a quiet engine. When a dog wants attention, it will jump all over you, lick you, or bark loudly and incessantly.

Example B
The pros and cons of allowing employers to pay teenagers less than the minimum wage

By allowing employers to pay teenagers less than the minimum wage, we expand the job market for teens. Employers who would not otherwise have the financial resources to hire an additional person might do so at a lower salary. Of course by opening up such lower-paying jobs, we cut many adults out of the job market. Many employers may choose the 17-year-old over the 35-year-old merely to save a few dollars a week.

Example C
The appropriate minimum drinking age

Twenty-one years is an appropriate age to officially begin drinking. That minimum age totally removes liquor from the high school scene, and eliminates the problem of high school seniors buying liquor and sharing it with younger students. At age twenty-one, most people are experienced drivers and are more aware of the dangers of drunken driving.

PRACTICE 6
Organized information
1. Enjoyed meeting you at the convention.
2. Presentation well planned and presented, great deal of information.
3. Excellent workshop.
4. *Prospectus* need.
5. Innovative and exciting ideas.
6. Please visit.
7. Thanks for valuable presentation.

Letter
Overseas Marketing
312 Main Street
Worcester, Massachusetts 01608
September 10, 2000

Ms. Eva Reyes, President
Dynamic Sales, Inc.
400 Lenox Avenue
Chicago, Illinois 60646

Dear Ms. Reyes:
I enjoyed meeting you at the National Sales Convention. Your presentation was extremely well planned and executed. My colleagues and I left with a great deal of practical information and strategies. Yours was one of the most valuable sessions I have ever attended.

The *Prospectus* you discussed clearly states your philosophy and activities, but unfortunately I did not get a copy at the convention. Would you please mail one to my office? Many of your ideas were innovative and exciting, and I am eager to begin implementing them in my district. Should you ever travel to Massachusetts, I would appreciate meeting with you and discussing how I have incorporated your theories into my work.

Again, thank you for a most valuable presentation.

Sincerely,
Rose Haber
Marketing Manager

4.

Get It Into Shape

If you have thought about what you want to write and why you are writing it, then you probably have a pretty good idea also of the overall form that your writing will take. For example, if you are writing to your representative in Congress, you'll be sending him or her a letter. If you are sending a coworker a message or request, you will want to put it down on paper as a memorandum. If you are compiling a summary of facts and opinions for school or office, you will be assembling a report. But each of these forms of writing has a structure of its own. The right format helps communicate your purpose and makes your writing reader-friendly.

General Rules for Format

Remember, your purpose in writing is to have your written material read. If your printed page looks overwhelming, it will sit indefinitely in someone's "things I'm going to read someday" pile. Here are five useful rules for turning out readable, attractive written material:

1. **Use white space.**
    * Do not think that single-spaced, top-to-bottom, side-to-side typing demonstrates hard work. It just makes reading difficult.
    * Double-space between paragraphs.
    * Indent material where appropriate.
    * Use margins to simplify reading.
2. **Use subheadings to separate unrelated material.**
3. **Use lists instead of sentences where possible.** Lists are easier to read and to retain.
4. **Use short paragraphs**—no more than seven lines, fewer if possible. First and last paragraphs, in particular, should be no more than five lines.
5. **Use bullets, numbers, or other devices to highlight items in a series:**
    √   ×   ◆

Letters

When do you write a letter? Letters are written to inform, request information, complain, praise, persuade, thank—in general, to communicate with another person through the mail. Letters can be formal, informal, even casual, depending upon your purpose and your relationship with your correspondent.

Letters, especially business letters, should follow a generally accepted form. This form assures that the letter arrives at the proper location, gives the necessary information in a concise way, and contains your name and address so the recipient can answer your letter easily. Figure 1 shows the basic elements of a business letter. We'll discuss these elements one at a time.

Placement

Standard letter format used to be as follows:

Your Address
Date

Recipient's Name and Title
Recipient's Address

Salutation
   Indent for paragraphs

Closing

Most business letters are now typed in a format known as flush left and block style:

Your Address
Date

Recipient's Name and Title
Recipient's Address

Salutation

No indent for paragraphs

Closing

Address:	From whom?
	Company Letterhead
	Above date or
	Below typed name
Date:	When?
Heading:	To whom?
	Name and Title
	Company
	Address
Salutation:	To whom?
	Dear . . .
Introduction:	One short paragraph states the subject or purpose of the letter.
Body:	One, two, three, or more paragraphs contain the relevant details.
Conclusion:	The conclusion should give direction. One short paragraph finishes the letter with a summary, a recommendation, an instruction, or a thank you.
Closing:	The appropriate good-bye.
Signature:	
Typed Name:	Jane Adams

FIGURE 1

Although both formats are acceptable, you should be consistent. Note that your address and the date must be on the same side of the page as the closing. You cannot have just one of these elements off to the right; they must balance one another.

Of course, printed stationery, business and personal, takes care of the inside address—often in a creative, nontraditional way.

Figure 2 follows this format. Read the letter and notice how the opening paragraph introduces the subject, the second paragraph details the incident and provides greater explanation, and the third paragraph concludes with mention of the excellent relationship the writer has had with the company to date and with a reminder that she expects reimbursement.

Now let's look at the several elements of a letter more carefully.

Your Address

Unless you are using personalized stationery, on which your name and address are printed, or you have a business letterhead (see Figure 3), type your address at the top of the paper, as shown in Figure 2. When writing to a close friend or relative, your more informal letter need not include the address; see Figure 4 for an example. However, if you meet someone casually, though on a friendly basis, and it is likely that the person does not know where you live, it is thoughtful to include your address in the letter.

The Date

In a formal letter, spell out the month, as shown in Figure 2. Even in an informal business letter, always spell out the month because it is clearer that way, and in business communications dates are often very important. Because so much business correspondence is international, and the day/month sequence of numerical dates varies among countries, writing out the month ensures clarity. If, on the other hand, you are writing to your mother in Florida, you can safely put the date in all numerals.

Inside Address

For all business or formal communication, include the name and address of the person to whom you are writing. In offices, the envelopes are opened by machine and mail is sorted in a mail room. If the address is only on the envelope, no one will know to whom the letter should go. The address includes the name, title or position of the person who should receive the letter, the company or organization, and the complete address of the organization. A friendly letter does not need the inside address because the envelope will be opened by the person to whom you have addressed the letter.

106 Goodtree Drive
Columbus, Ohio 43201
February 10, 2000

Mr. Brian Jaffee, President
Cool-It, Inc.
738 Second Avenue
New York, New York 10017

Dear Mr. Jaffee:

On January 23, 2000, while a local Cool-It, Inc. representative was servicing my air conditioner, the tank of Freon exploded in my basement. The tank was located next to my clothes dryer; thus this explosion caused damage to my dryer as well as to some clothing that was in the dryer at the time. This event led to an expensive dryer service call and the need to replace a complete load of laundry. I would appreciate full reimbursement for the items listed on the attached bills.

The serviceman who repaired the dryer suggested that the malfunction was mostly caused by the Freon. The spilled Freon permanently froze the dryer thermostat, preventing the dryer from cooling down. A full load of towels and underwear that were in the dryer at the time became excessively dried out to the point of disintegration. In fact, when I removed the laundry from the dryer, the laundry fell apart in my hands. Before the explosion, the load of laundry was fine and the dryer worked perfectly.

I've always had an excellent relationship with your company and look forward to your continuing service. Your representative, by the way, was courteous and thorough in his job of repairing the air-conditioning system. I look forward to your payment within a reasonable amount of time.

Thank you.

Sincerely,

Paula De Meo

FIGURE 2

ABC Corporation

231 West 53rd Street, New York, New York 10022

July 10, 2000

Ms. Cary Jeffers
66 Columbus Avenue
Tarrytown, New York 10571

Dear Ms. Jeffers:

Thank you for your letter (dated June 25, 2000) asking about employment possibilities at the ABC Corporation. We receive a number of such requests each year, and must therefore limit interviews to individuals with prior work experience. Your résumé indicates that you have no such prior experience, and therefore I cannot offer you any hope at this time. However, should you still want to work for our company after having gained a few years' experience in the field, we would be most happy to reconsider your application.

Thank you for considering ABC Corporation. We wish you luck in securing employment very soon.

Very truly yours,

David Green
Personnel Director

DG/sl

FIGURE 3

8/4/2000

Dear Ellen,

Colorado is beautiful at this time of year—at least, as much as I've seen of it. It has been raining since we arrived four days ago, but that's okay. Susan has had a chance to let her sprained ankle heal and Mickey's sore throat is almost gone.

Our evenings have been eventful. I am awakened each night at about 2 A.M. by "Lady Macbeth." Linda has been getting these horrible nosebleeds, and she wanders into my room for help. I'm sure she just has to get used to the altitude.

I understand the swimming, hiking, and shopping are marvelous here. I hope I get out of the apartment soon.

Love to everyone.

Love,

FIGURE 4

Greeting

The rule is simple: letters begin "Dear (Name)." But the reality is more difficult. Awareness of sexism in language has led to changes in custom. A decade ago, if you were addressing an unknown person or company in general, the greeting you would have used was "Gentlemen." That is no longer the case. Most likely the company or department will include women. When you have an unidentified or mixed group to address, use "Ladies and Gentlemen." If addressing an unknown individual whose title you know, use a greeting such as "Dear Personnel Director." If you don't know the title, "Dear Sir/Madam" will do.

A major problem arises when you must answer a letter from someone whose name gives no clue to the signer's sex. A letter signed by S. Khang or Pat McEnroy will not help. In this instance, use the available information: "Dear S. Khang" or "Dear Pat McEnroy."

If you are on a first-name basis with your business correspondent, it is appropriate to address the letter using that person's first name, as in "Dear Emily." Note that the colon is not replaced by a comma in a business letter. If your letter were a personal one—say, to your aunt about a planned Christmas party—you would address her with the first name and follow that name with a comma.

Here are some standard greetings for business correspondence:
Gentlemen:
Dear Sir:
Dear Sirs:
Dear Mr. Yasuda:
Dear Ms. Barry:
Dear Dr. Gandhi:
Dear Director of Personnel:
Dear Salespeople:
Ladies and Gentlemen:

Some examples of greetings for friendly letters:
Dear Uncle Bob,
Dear Maria,
Dearest Michael,
Dear S. Gomez:
Dear Company B:
Dear Emily:

The Body of the Letter

Since your opening paragraph is like a first meeting with your reader, the impression you make is a lasting one. The reader expects you to reveal your purpose clearly. Whether it is to complain, compliment, or inform, it should be apparent immediately.

To clearly state the purpose and details of your message, have a plan in mind when you begin. You may need to make only a few notes, but for a longer, more complicated communication you will probably want to write an outline (see Chapter 2). Write a first draft and then put it aside for a few hours. When you return, you will not only find any errors you may have made in grammar, word choice, or facts, but you will also be able to check the tone of your letter. Even a letter expressing dissatisfaction should not be nasty or rude. Remember that when your letter goes into the mail—with your signature on it—it becomes a written record of your thoughts. You will be accountable for what it says, so a second check of the facts and figures will ensure accuracy and help you avoid having to send a clarifying letter or apology.

Say what you want, clearly and concisely. Your letter may be long, but it should not ramble. Every sentence should be a necessary one. The traditional newspaper reporter questions will help you keep on track. Answer the questions who? what? when? where? and why? and you will probably give all the necessary information.

Just as your first impression is lasting, so is your final one. Make sure your reader knows what you expect. If you plan a follow-up phone call, say so and say when it will arrive. If you want a written or telephone response, ask for it. If you began the letter by thanking the person, reinforce your appreciation in the final paragraph.

Closings

Closings can range from "Love" to "Very truly yours," depending upon the purpose of your letter. The closing should be in the same style as the greeting. A letter would not begin with "Dear Sir:" and end with "Love." Standard punctuation form requires a comma after the closing.

> Some formal closings are:
>> Very truly yours,
>> Sincerely,
>> Yours truly,
>
> Some friendly closings are:
>> Fondly,
>> Love,
>> Best regards,
>> As ever,

Name and Signature

If your letter is business correspondence, the standard form is to follow the closing with your name and title (see Figure 3), and then sign the letter, with your name and title typed beneath the signature. If you are writing a business letter as a consumer (for example, if you are writing your local power company regarding a mistake on their bill), you have no company name to include. In that case, just sign your name below the closing and then type your name beneath the signature (see Figure 2).

A Final Reminder

Your letter may include correct facts and well-written paragraphs, but if it doesn't look polished, your reader will be distracted from the contents. The letter should be typed neatly, properly spaced on good-quality bond paper. If it is a business letter, you should retain a copy for your files. If you cannot type your letter, take pains to write neatly and to follow correct form. Personal letters, of course, may be handwritten on stationery or the paper of your choice.

Purpose plays a role in determining whether to type or handwrite a note. A handwritten thank-you note, for example, demonstrates more warmth than a typed letter.

PRACTICE 1

Write the following letters. Remember to follow the correct format.

1. You are Maria Borges, Finance Chairperson for the United Bank of Connecticut, which is located at 1115 Fairfield Avenue in Hartford 06120. You are requesting information about a banking seminar scheduled in July in Montreal, Canada M5V 2TI. The seminar is being sponsored by the International Banking Association, which is located at 214 White Road in Montreal. The training director is Susanne Murat.
2. You are Alina Paz, a teenager in Madison, Wisconsin 53721. You live at 4 Elm Street. A relative who lives in New York has just been promoted to Department Chairperson for the Mathematics Department at New York University. Your relative, Elsie Paz, lives at 609 West 59th Street in New York 10021. You are writing to introduce yourself and establish your familial connection, in the hope she can help get you admitted to the university for graduate work. You will be in New York City next month and would like to meet with her.

Memorandums

Letters are one form of communication—the standard form when the communications are transmitted through the mails. A memorandum is more commonly used in interoffice communications for sharing information, setting procedures, or asking questions within a company or organization. Every business has its preferred style for memos, but the tips that follow can be applied in most situations. Treat a memo as you would any other kind of writing; that is, plan ahead and then construct clear and concise sentences that convey your intentions. Either write a brief outline or jot down phrases that will help you organize your thinking. Stick to the one subject at hand. State your purpose first; then give all the necessary facts. Tell what you want done or request information. If you are informing the reader, do so simply and clearly, keeping your tone friendly and positive. A memo need not be an edict. Simply answer the question, "What do I want to say?" Again, make sure that what you say is accurate because memos, when filed, become records.

Although a memo is very much like a letter in purpose, its structure is different. A memo usually has the format shown in Figure 5.

TO:	To whom are you writing? Give name and title.
FROM:	Your name and title.
DATE:	When?
SUBJECT:	A brief, clear reference.
Purpose:	Why are you writing the memo?
Relevant Details:	What must the recipient know?
Closure:	What must the recipient do?
Thank You and/or Availability:	Thank recipient and offer to answer questions.

ADC:df

Distribution

FIGURE 5

Traditionally, a memo is not signed at the bottom the way a letter would be. Instead, the sender initials the memo next to his or her name at the top. Many companies, however, now have a signature line at the bottom of memos and require a full signature. The SUBJECT line should be informative, summing up the subject matter in a few words. For example, if the memo is to a coworker requesting reassignment of parking spaces in the company lot, the SUBJECT line would be "SUBJECT: New Company Parking Spaces."

Note the structure of the memo in Figure 6. The opening gets right to the point. Helms recalls that she and Macaulay have agreed that there is a potential problem and then proposes a solution. For emphasis, the solution is set off—highlighted—in its own paragraph. Other ways to visually emphasize ideas include using numbers, letters, headings, or bullets (black dots) at the left-hand margin. The final two sentences of Helms's memo tell Macaulay what to do and thank him for his cooperation.

Note also that job titles appear next to the names. These titles can be omitted in very informal memos (see Figure 7). Other memos, which will be filed for future reference, should have the titles included.

Now read the memo in Figure 8. Does it meet all the requirements of a well-written memo? Yes. This short memo gets the job done. The subject is clearly stated in the SUBJECT line. In the first sentence, the reader learns the new due date and what has to be done. Sentences 2 and 3 show the writer's concern for Suni's well-being. There is nothing wrong with a personal touch. One improvement would be to include the job titles and/or department names.

MEMORANDUM

TO: William Macaulay, V.P., Marketing
FROM: Rebecca Helms, Purchasing Agent
DATE: April 10, 2000
SUBJECT: Purchase Agreement Number 42

When we met last Tuesday, we concurred that the above purchase agreement #42 was vague and could lead to problems once the job is completed. I propose the following change:
1.   Delete lines 4–7.
2.   Insert the following in place of lines 4–7:
"The seller is under no obligation to accept returned merchandise 90 days after delivery." Let me know within 2 days if you agree with this change. Thank you.

MEMO
TO: Carol
FROM: Sue
DATE: May 3, 2000
SUBJECT: 1990 Dead Files

You and I are responsible for transferring last year's files to the warehouse. I'm available any morning next week. Please let me know the day and time convenient for you.

FIGURES 6 & 7

FROM THE DESK OF JOHN SMITH:
TO: Suni Kim
DATE: December 10, 2000
SUBJECT: Monthly Report

You should be pleased to know that your December monthly report will not be due until January 7, 2001. This extension should make your vacation a little more relaxing. Enjoy the holidays.

MEMO
TO: Martin Atkins, Director of Rehabilitation Services
FROM: Elias Korb, M.D., Hospital Administrator
DATE: November 10, 2000
SUBJECT: Development of a hortitherapy program for patients

At the recent Hospital Directors' Round Table, Dr. Seymour Watson of the New England Hortitherapy Council gave a speech on the positive results achieved with hospitalized patients who had been taking care of plants. He further explained the long-term benefits of hortitherapy, especially its continued use after the patient's discharge.

Dr. Watson gave me some guidelines on raising funds for such a project. I'm going to survey the board to see how much money could be made available for our own hortitherapy program.

I've attached Dr. Watson's studies, "The Use of Hortitherapy in Geriatric Settings," "Hortitherapy in a Psychiatric Setting," and "Outpatient Programs in Hortitherapy." Please study these and decide which approach we could use at Sunnycrest.

After you decide which patients would benefit most from the program, estimate what personnel and supplies would cost for 20 patients. I'll need your cost estimates by December 16, 2000, so that I can review them before presenting my report to the Board of Directors on December 30.

FIGURES 8 & 9

The memo in Figure 7 is a very informal one between two coworkers. No last names appear in the heading, and without these names, the memo would be almost useless as a record. Sue gets to the point immediately, however, noting co-responsibility for moving the files and letting Carol know the times during the week that she will be available. Sue then tells Carol what to do—that is, to decide on a convenient time to work together.

Sometimes you will need to write a longer memo. For example, you may want to provide background information related to the subject, as well as give current information. Read Figure 9 and note how the need dictates form. In this memo, the introduction explains the background of Dr. Korb's idea. The next part of the memo tells what the writer intends to do. The memo then asks Martin Atkins, the reader, to do three things: read, select, and estimate. What Martin Atkins has to do is detailed as well. The memo concludes with a due date. It is effective and should result in Dr. Korb's getting what he wants.

PRACTICE 2

Select two of the following three situations and write an appropriate memo for each.
1. From the supervisor of a department to an employee who is consistently late.
2. From a supervisor in the order department to the inventory control manager, noting a shortage in a recent shipment to a key client.
3. From a supervisor who plans to be away to an employee designated to cover that supervisor's duties during that time.

Reports and Proposals

Letters and memorandums are very common forms of writing, but there are other instances when you will write, too. In school you may already have written book reports and themes on a variety of subjects. A report is a detailed statement of accomplishments or findings. A proposal is a request for funding to solve a recognized problem or for permission to implement a new idea.

Since reports and proposals serve different functions, they take on different forms. Regardless of the format, however, the basics of good writing prevail. You should present your information in a clear, concise style. You need to document your facts, and if you are taking facts from another source, you must give credit to those sources. In a formal report for school, you would use footnotes. For a business report, you would include footnotes where appropriate. Your conclusions should be set off from your facts, so the reader is able to distinguish fact from opinion. In lengthier reports, it is often helpful to include a summary at the beginning so that the reader can know at the start the scope and breadth of the report without having to first read the entire report.

Reports

Most reports have a set form, similar to an outline. For example, a business report may follow this format:

Cover page:	title, author, readers, date of report
Summary or abstract:	a brief overview of the subject covered and conclusions drawn
Introduction:	a beginning section in which you set the scene, giving relevant background information and/or explaining terminology used in the report
Body:	the information you are sharing, which supports the conclusions you have drawn
Appendix:	all additional relevant data, such as sources of information, additional charts and graphs, and supporting statistics

In preparing reports for business, check for company style by referring to previous reports. For school reports, ask your teacher what particulars are important to him or her. No one form is correct, but you should use the form preferred.

A lengthy report should have a cover page indicating the title of the report, the person or persons to whom it is submitted, the person or persons by whom it is submitted, and the date. The table of contents indicates the scope of the report and the organization of the body of the report. Note the cover page, table of contents, and excerpt from the introduction of a report, shown as Figure 10.

As an example of style, we have included as Figure 11 an excerpt from a report on critical thinking in education. This excerpt shows the use of a footnote, as well as a listing of points, with bullets to emphasize the listing.

REPORT*
OF THE
JOINT STATEWIDE TASK FORCE ON PRE-COLLEGE PREPARATION

Submitted to:
Saul Cooperman
Commissioner of Education

and

T. Edward Hollander
Chancellor of Higher Education

by:

The Joint Statewide Task Force on Pre-College Preparation
December, 1983

*Used with permission of state of New Jersey Department of Higher Education.

FIGURE 10

TABLE OF CONTENTS

I. INTRODUCTION AND OVERVIEW

The problems facing our schools and colleges are many. These problems have been well documented, and recommendations for change have been developed by a multitude of committees, task forces, and special commissions both in New Jersey and across the nation.

This report focuses on precollege preparation in English and mathematics, only one aspect, albeit an important aspect, of a national effort to improve quality of education in this country. Our argument is based upon the assertion that the primary mission of all educational institutions is to promote learning. We recommend concrete steps that should be taken to enhance the intellectual development and academic performance of students who come to learn. We propose a plan of action that promises better education for the generations to come.

Since the mid-1970s, there has been a growing public perception that students are graduating from the nation's secondary schools lacking proficiency in English and mathematics. This perception has been reinforced by annual publication of the results of nationwide testing programs, such as the Scholastic Aptitude Tests of the College Board. Within this state, results of the New Jersey College Basic Skills Placement Test provide continuing evidence that many students entering the state's colleges are deficient in English and mathematics. Colleges and universities have found it necessary to establish remedial programs in English and mathematics; many high schools and elementary schools have shifted their focus to emphasize development of these proficiencies.

The College Board through its Educational Equality Project and systems of higher education in such states as California, Ohio, Kentucky, and Louisiana have attempted to define the skills college-bound students should be able to demonstrate in preparation for college-level course work. In spring 1982 New Jersey determined to make a similar effort. Each sector of New Jersey's higher education community developed a set of recommendations focused upon the pre-college preparation of students in English and mathematics. These sector reports became the starting point for the work of this Statewide Task Force on Pre-College Preparation.

Appointed in the spring of 1983 as a joint effort between the Departments of Education and Higher Education, the Task Force was charged by Commissioner Saul Cooperman and Chancellor T. Edward Hollander to consider the following issues:

1) college preparatory curricula in secondary schools and admission requirements in English and mathematics at the state university and at the state colleges;

2) skills proficiencies in English and mathematics that students should be able to demonstrate in order to undertake college-level coursework;

3) the relationships and distinctions between "remedial" and "baccalaureate level" work in English and mathematics, and the application of these definitions to the transfer of credits between two-year and four-year institutions; and,

4) means of using available resources more effectively to improve the pre-college preparation of students in English and mathematics in order to minimize the need for remediation in the colleges.

The scope of our report is limited, quite properly, by the charge given to the Task Force. We have concentrated primarily on the areas of English and mathematics with emphasis on the high school level.

FIGURE 10

The Importance of Critical Thinking and Reasoning

While we focus here on specific, detailed skills, we wish to emphasize the important role of critical thinking and reasoning in the students' educational development. Although it may be more difficult to teach or to evaluate, the ability to think clearly, to understand, is an obvious necessity for quality education.

Although no exhaustive set of sub-skills cumulatively constitutes proficiency in critical thinking and reasoning, there are certain identifiable abilities, including:

- the ability to identify and formulate problems, as well as the ability to propose and evaluate ways to solve them;
- the ability to recognize and use inductive and deductive reasoning, and to recognize fallacies in reasoning;
- the ability to draw reasonable conclusions from information found in various sources whether written, spoken, or displayed in tables or graphs, and to defend one's conclusions rationally;
- the ability to comprehend, develop, and use concepts and generalizations;
- the ability to distinguish between fact and opinion.*

This emphasis on the importance of critical thinking and reasoning proficiencies, however, does not mean that knowledge of facts is unnecessary or unimportant. Indeed, critical thinking and reasoning depend upon a command of factual information as well as the ability to analyze it. Thus, students should be expected both to acquire information and to use it in reasoning their way through.

*Educational Equality Project's "Academic Preparation for College," College Board, 1983

FIGURE 11

Proposals

Proposals are requests for funding or for permission to implement a new idea. They follow the same general approach as a report, although most proposals have their own form. Among different companies or agencies, the requested format will vary; one typical form follows:

Abstract or summary:	a brief overview of the proposal
Statement of need:	a brief explanation of why the program or system is necessary
Goals and objectives:	detailed explanation of what will be accomplished by implementing the proposal
Implementation:	a plan for putting the program into action, including detailed information on necessary staff, materials, time, equipment, and how these will be used
Budget:	a breakdown of costs involved
Evaluation procedure:	a summary view of the proposal and how it will be evaluated in the end

Figure 12 is an example of an abstract from a proposal. Figure 13 is a narrative of goals and objectives.

A commonly accepted form for stating objectives follows:

Objective	Activity	Evaluation
1. Students will improve basic skills.	1.1 One-to-one instruction.	1.1 Student improvement as measured by informal and formal assessment.
	1.2 Small-group instruction in reading and math.	1.2 Student improvement as measured by informal and formal assessment.
	1.3 Development of materials to meet specific student needs.	Student improvement through use of targeted materials.
2. Students will improve self-image.	2.1 One-to-one counseling.	2.1 Student performance. Student responses to counselor. Student responses to formal questionnaire.
	2.2 Positive reinforcement of progress.	2.2 Student attendance. Student performance. Student responses to formal questionnaire.

ABSTRACT

There is a growing awareness in the field of Adult Basic Education of some adults having learning disabilities that were neither diagnosed nor treated when they were younger. The general attitude in the existing corps of child-oriented Learning Disabilities Specialists is that it is too late to deal with these problems. Many adult educators are realizing that it is *never too late.*

Among the programs offered at the Union County Regional Adult Learning Center are an Adult Basic Education program and a High School Completion program. We find that the ABE students are divided into two distinct groups:

1. Those who would be able to move into HSC with time and effort, who could work on their own and in groups.
2. Those who have not mastered the most basic skills in reading or math and need and demand constant one-to-one attention.

This second group needs a special program of instruction and counseling geared specifically to build up skills and egos.

This proposal offers a total-person package. We hope to identify specific problems, treat them as thoroughly as possible, and offer alternative solutions where necessary. We intend to help the learning disabled adult recognize his/her disabilities as such, learn to deal with or around them effectively, improve his/her basic educational skills, his/her employability, and his/her self-image.

FIGURE 12

II. PROJECT GOAL(S) AND OPERATIONAL OBJECTIVES

It is our belief, as well as that of our staff and colleagues throughout the state, that with proper diagnosis and individualized instruction the learning disabled, functionally illiterate adult will

a) improve his/her basic skills.
b) improve his/her self-image.
c) become employable or capable of higher employment.

Our proposed program would include testing students who give any indication at all of having a learning problem and developing a delivery system of remediation and education. While working on eliminating, minimizing, or compensating for a learning problem, the student will have a parallel program of instruction. Concurrently, we would offer developmental counseling on a group and individual basis to repair the damaged self-image of the learning disabled adult, to help him/her accept his/her condition and to aid him/her in developing an awareness of an opportunity to improve.

Learning materials will be developed in conjunction with each student's prescription. Also, existing published and teacher-made ABE materials will be used where applicable.

FIGURE 13

Personalized Style Sheet for Your Use

Chapters 6 through 9 are specific, skill-building chapters. As you work through the exercises in each, you will identify your personal areas for writing improvement. These will range from sentence structure to grammar, punctuation, and vocabulary building. Use the Personalized Style Sheet on the following page to note the areas on which you should work. We will ask you to return to this sheet before you attempt the exercises in Chapter 11.

Below is an example of a personalized style sheet showing one writer's specific problems in grammar and punctuation.

Personalized Style Sheet

Name:	Jennifer Taylor
Rule:	Pronouns must agree.
Example:	If <u>I</u> talk to different people, <u>I</u> get a different perspective; When <u>I</u> talk with managers, <u>I</u> get a different perspective.
Rule:	Introductory words, phrases, and clauses should be followed by commas.
Example:	Next, we installed a word processing program. When I accepted this position, I assumed my authority would be equal to my responsibility.
Rule:	<u>Someone</u> is singular.
Example (incorrect):	Someone doesn't leave <u>their</u> (plural) paper.
Example (correct):	Someone left <u>his/her</u> paper on the table.
Rule:	<u>Who</u> performs the action in a sentence.
Example:	<u>Who</u> can help with this project?

Personalized Style Sheet

Name: _____

ANSWERS

Your responses will not be exactly the same as those that follow. The answer key provides samples. Do your answers offer the same facts and follow the correct form? How closely do your responses match the tone in the samples?

PRACTICE 1

1.
United Bank of Connecticut
1115 Fairfield Avenue
Hartford, Connecticut 06120
June 2, 2000

Ms. Susanne Murat, Training Director
International Banking Association
214 White Road
Montreal, Canada M5V 2TI

Dear Ms. Murat:

   I am planning to attend the seminar your Association is sponsoring in July. Please send me program and registration information as soon as possible. Thank you for your immediate reply.

Sincerely,

Maria Borges
Finance Chairperson

2.

4 Elm Street
Madison, Wisconsin 53721
April 10, 2000

Ms. Elsie Paz
609 West 59th Street
New York, New York 10021

Dear Aunt Elsie,

Congratulations on your recent promotion to Department Chairperson at New York University. Our whole family in Madison is very proud of you.

You might not remember me from the last time we met, because at that time I was only a tyke of 4 years. Since then, I've grown up and am currently enrolled at the University of Wisconsin, expecting to get my bachelor's degree next June. I'm a mathematics major, and I am planning to apply to the graduate mathematics program at New York University. I've gotten all the application forms, and I am hoping you might be able to recommend me for admission to the program. Could we meet next month when I will be in New York? I look forward to seeing you again.

Love,
Alina

PRACTICE 2

1.
TO: John Smith
FROM: Manuel Garcia
DATE: July 9, 2000
SUBJECT: Consistent Tardiness

As you know, our agency opens at 9 A.M. and clients are waiting to be served each day as the doors open. I have informed you repeatedly, in person and in memos, of my requirement that all employees be available at 8:45 A.M. You have yet to be in the office before 9:15 A.M. Should you arrive later than 8:45 A.M. on one more occasion, I will have to assume that you either cannot or will not comply with the stated starting time and I will be forced to terminate your employment.

2.
TO: Rafael Ortega, Inventory Control Manager
FROM: Sally Farmer, Supervisor, Order Department
DATE: October 10, 2000
SUBJECT: ORDER #67-8850/October 1, 2000

Please note that the above order was shipped short of 50 copies of WRITING THE EASY WAY. This customer is one of our key buyers, and expects a replacement shipment within two days. Can you look into this and assure me that the shipment will go out immediately via Federal Express?

3.
TO: William
FROM: Rita
DATE: February 16, 2001
SUBJECT: My upcoming vacation—2/23–2/30

Please read the attached outline of duties in its entirety before I leave on Tuesday. I will be available to answer any questions you might have regarding materials, personnel, etc. Please maintain a log of messages, and note which ones will not have been answered. John should be available to assist you when necessary. Thank you for taking on the extra load; I'll be available for same when your vacation comes along.

5.

Develop Powerful Paragraphs _____

A *paragraph* is a group of sentences about one topic. Traditionally, the first line of each new paragraph is indented about an inch, to let the reader know that a new topic is about to be discussed. Block style, with no indentation, is common in business writing; however, a double space between the paragraphs indicates a break between ideas or topics.

What is the importance of this information to you as a writer? The answer is clear: in every paragraph you write, develop one idea fully, and don't wander from that topic to another one. It is unfair to your readers, for instance, to start a paragraph with *fossils* as your topic and to finish with *volcanic eruptions* as the central thought.

As you read the following paragraph, think about the one idea that the writer develops. What is that idea?

> Research shows that habits and lifestyle in the 1990s were a greater risk to our health than any other factor. Where pneumonia and diphtheria took their toll in the nineteenth century, smoking, poor diet, and drinking exacted their toll in the twentieth. These poor habits greatly increased our chances of developing cancer and heart disease or of dying in an auto accident.

Explanation: The writer states the topic in the first sentence: our habits and lifestyle, not other factors, put our health at risk. The rest of the paragraph supports that statement. The paragraph explains what some of the risks used to be (pneumonia and diphtheria) in the nineteenth century and what they became (smoking, poor diet, drinking) in the twentieth century. The last sentence tells what life-threatening results our habits can lead to.

Each paragraph must focus on one idea. Sometimes this idea can be expressed in one sentence: "Thank you for considering this request." Usually a paragraph contains at least three sentences. In business communications, however, more than five or six sentences create paragraphs that invite skimming. In any case, if you want your writing read, keep your paragraphs to a manageable length.

PRACTICE 1

Read these paragraphs. In each case the writer develops one idea. State that idea in your own words.

1. Computers have not only changed how fighters fly; they have also changed the demands on the men who will be flying them. In the past, pilots had to be taught the system. Now many trained technicians or systems operators also know how to fly. This is not to say that bespectacled prodigies, weighing 95 pounds and carrying texts on advanced computer technology in one hand and Dramamine in the other, are about to start coming out of fighter pilot school. As long as pilots are needed in fighters—which may not be much longer—the emphasis will be on physically fit individuals with excellent sight and very sound reflexes. But from now on, fighter pilots will also tend to have engineering and technical backgrounds.

Topic: _____

2. Our business plan should answer two important questions: how is our business doing right now, and where do we want the business to be in five years' time? To write the plan, we'll have to take a careful look at such factors as our current products, our financial needs and resources, and our management policies. A critical look at the company's strengths and weaknesses will enable us to develop strategies to reach our long-term goals.

Topic: _____

The Topic Sentence

The topic sentence states the main idea of the paragraph. A topic sentence often opens the paragraph. Two good reasons for that placement exist. First, the writer can easily develop the topic in the following sentences. Second, the reader receives the most important idea immediately; placed first, the topic sentence prepares the reader for what is to come. In business writing, this approach is particularly useful because busy executives often want to skim through a paragraph to get the main idea quickly. For example, read the following paragraph:

Community leaders can take an active part in slowing down demand for water and seeing that it is not poisoned. To begin, leaders can set up conservation programs to educate the public. They can enact measures to conserve water in public schools, hospitals, and other buildings. In addition, they can change the pricing system to discourage high-volume water use, as well as identify the high-water users in industry and help them develop conservation plans. Finally, community leaders can try to convince people and industry not to poison the water we have left.

Were you able to locate the topic sentence in the paragraph above? Underline it and notice where it is in the paragraph.

The topic doesn't have to be stated in the first sentence, however. Sometimes the topic sentence is more effective later in the paragraph. If the topic sentence appears in the middle of the paragraph, for instance, the writer can use the opening sentence as a transition from the preceding paragraph. If a topic sentence comes at the end, the paragraph builds to a climax, holding the reader's interest until the last sentence. Experienced writers know that, if every paragraph begins with the topic sentence, they have to work very hard to maintain the reader's interest. Except in business writing, therefore, the best advice is to vary your approach, with topic sentences appearing at the beginning, in the middle, and at the end.

PRACTICE 2

Underline the topic sentence in each paragraph.

1

Reproduction, of course, is the key to an organism's survival. Failure to reproduce means no progeny. If this continues, it means an end to the species. And offspring must be produced in sufficient numbers so that some few will survive all threats of their environment. So salmon must lay 28 million eggs in one season while oysters must produce four times that amount to survive their predators and other risks and maintain their species in the world.

2

But installing telephone service for anyone who wants it is no longer our only interest. The newest developments in telecommunications—including information sharing—offer more exciting possibilities. We predict that our company will soon be able to link up your home or office with the worldwide information explosion.

3

Now that you've determined your purpose for writing, and know who your reader will be, you're ready to write some research notes. Used in the following way, a card system will keep your notes organized and prevent your retracing steps. Use at least two cards for each publication. Use the first card to record the title, author, publisher, page number, catalog number, and date of publication for each book or periodical. Be sure to give each card a cross-reference number. Then, on your second (third, fourth, etc.) card, along with your research, write the cross-reference number from your title card.

4

This year we need to assess the impact that an aging population will have on our business. An intense interest in leisure-time activity and the money to spend on it make this the market to capture. On the other hand, an aging population requires a more comfortable environment and less strenuous activities.

5

This geography, harsh climate, different languages, and divergent cultures often make that land seem less like a single nation and more like a conservative collection of feuding fiefdoms. Quebec has its own vibrant culture and celebrities who are virtually unknown next door in Ontario and vice versa. Canada's politically underrepresented West resents the economic dominance of central Canada, which is jealous of the West's oil and gas. Every region tells ethnic jokes about the residents of Newfoundland, Canada's newest province, where they refer to people from other provinces disparagingly as C.F.A.'s (Come From Aways).

6

Successful business trainers say that the most important component of a business letter is its friendly tone. A friendly tone makes the message more acceptable no matter what it is. When you make the effort to use a conversational tone, your writing is likely to be clearer, too.

7

Take the advice of the Social Security Administration and periodically check the agency's record of your earnings. Because most of us give no thought at all to our contributions until it is time to collect them, we're unaware of what can go wrong. Errors are made occasionally and these result in lower retirement benefits. It is easier to check your earnings record every few years than to unravel the mystery of missing benefits when you are ready to retire.

Purpose: First, Last, and Always

Just when you thought you'd never hear it again, here is another reminder: purpose is everything—or nearly everything. As we said in Chapter 1, when you know *why* you're writing something—to inform, to persuade, to motivate to action—you are more likely to organize your thoughts effectively. When you are editing your work, ask yourself, "How does this paragraph fit in with the purpose of my report, letter, or memo?" Furthermore, every paragraph should have the characteristics of a report as a whole: a purpose, a topic, and supporting ideas that develop the topic.

Below is a paragraph from a health report whose main purpose is to inform the reader about the dangerous effects of the sun's ultraviolet rays. Keep three questions in mind as you read the paragraph: 1. Is the purpose of the paragraph to persuade, inform, or motivate? 2. Do you think this paragraph advances the purpose of the report? Explain. 3. Which sentence states the topic?

> Ultraviolet radiation from the sun can reach you and burn your skin even if you're not directly in the sunlight. If you love to sunbathe, you should know that 80 percent of ultraviolet radiation can get through a layer of clouds. A beach umbrella will only partially protect you, because ultraviolet rays reflect off the sand. Even light beach clothing allows 25 percent of the ultraviolet rays to reach your skin. Don't count on a swim to shield you either, since 50 percent of the sun's ultraviolet radiation will reach those parts of your body that are underwater.

Let's answer the three questions stated above. The purpose of the paragraph is to inform. The paragraph ties directly into the overall purpose of the report because readers need to know how ultraviolet radiation reaches them in order to avoid the dangerous rays. The paragraph gives information that dispels myths about protection from the sun. Finally, the writer gets right to the point by stating the topic in the first sentence.

What's Your Plan?

Paragraphs don't just happen. Writing each paragraph calls for some careful preparation on your part. The first step is to identify your topic and then state it in a topic sentence. The next step is to select details to support, or back up, the topic so that your paragraph will be adequately developed and unified. A *well-developed paragraph* provides enough information to explain the topic in a meaningful way: it doesn't leave the reader hanging in midair, unsure of the point the writer is making. In a *unified paragraph*, every idea presented is directly related to the topic sentence.

As you draft your topic sentence, keep in mind the *plan of development* that you will be using when you write the paragraph. The way you word your topic sentence and the type of details you include in the paragraph will depend on the plan you have chosen. Sticking to this plan will make it easier for you to develop your ideas and will help keep the paragraph unified.

There are a number of different plans that writers use:

- Give examples that explain or support the topic sentence.
- Defend the opinion stated in the topic sentence.
- Compare and contrast two items or ideas stated in the topic sentence.
- Describe chronologically, or in time order, what the topic sentence states.
- Define a word or explain a process stated in the topic sentence.
- Link the topic sentence to an earlier topic or one to come.

Following are examples of different kinds of paragraph development. Before you read the explanation that follows each paragraph, decide what you think the writer's plan was. Use the list above to name each plan.

1. A substance grown from molds ushered in the age of antibiotics. An English bacteriologist, Alexander Fleming, discovered penicillin in 1928 when some mold he was growing fell from a culture plate. Fleming noticed that the mold had destroyed the bacteria around it. Following up on his accidental discovery, Fleming grew the mold on broth. Then he placed drops of the broth into test tubes containing disease-carrying bacteria. The broth stopped the bacteria's growth. Fleming called the broth penicillin. Later, the term was applied only to the active chemical substance formed in the broth. In 1940, two other scientists, Howard W. Florey and Ernst Chain, discovered how penicillin could be purified for use.

Plan _____

Paragraph 1 is developed chronologically; that is, events are described in the order in which they took place. Two dates stand out: 1928 in the second sentence and 1940 in the last sentence. Indeed, the paragraph records the history of penicillin, beginning with the discovery of some mold that had accidentally fallen from a culture plate. The paragraph also contains several words that act as clues to the chronological pattern. *Following, then,* and *later* all move the paragraph along in a time sequence.

2. We prefer technical schools that accept students from a variety of backgrounds. The school should welcome high school juniors and seniors who are prepared to tackle both the academic and the technical courses. High school graduates who choose vocational training instead of college would also benefit from the technical school's curriculum. And possibly the most important program in the school would be for men and women in their early twenties who have had low-paying jobs and are ready to come back to school to learn a trade.

Plan _____

In Paragraph 2, the writer states a preference in the topic sentence: We prefer technical schools that accept students from a variety of backgrounds. Each sentence that follows describes one of those backgrounds. Sentences two, three, and four offer *examples that support the topic sentence.*

3. The characteristics that help a plant survive in a particular environment are called adaptations. For example, only certain plants can adapt to the desert environment. The barrow cactus's structure allows it to gather water through its widespread root system after an infrequent rainstorm. Furthermore, the cactus's fleshy stem is well adapted to store a large amount of water.

Plan _____

In Paragraph 3, the topic sentence *defines* the term *adaptations;* the remaining sentences describe *adaptation* in a particular type of plant.

Now try your hand at identifying paragraph plans in the following practice exercise.

PRACTICE 3

Label each paragraph according to its plan. Use the list on page 00 to name each plan.

1. While discount telephone services can reduce a company's long-distance telephone expenses, they do not take into account two important factors. First, telephone companies throughout the country have converted to message unit billing, which means that local calls are no longer "free" and instead are billed as toll charges according to the length of conversation. As message-unit billing has expanded nationwide, more and more telephone users have begun to feel the heavy burden of local toll charges, charges that cannot be reduced with discount telephone service carriers. Second, since they cannot change the habits of telephone users, discount communications services by themselves are not totally effective in reducing toll charges. People are not generally prudent in the way they use the telephone. This is particularly true in business, where company phones are often used for personal calls and where business-related calls are overextended.

2. In my opinion, book censorship is a foolish and wasteful practice. Students can easily find these forbidden books elsewhere. Yet, we deprive readers of adequate teaching that would enlarge their thinking about the controversial contents of these books. We forget that qualified teachers not only instruct about literary styles, but also present the social attitudes of the times together with the author's intent, allowing the student to understand the book's controversial nature.

3. You won't impress any prospective employer who advertises a job if you send the same standard cover letter to all. Instead, read each ad for the qualifications required. Start your letter by stating an accomplishment of yours that corresponds to those qualifications. Finally, relate your sincere interest in the job to the stated accomplishment.

4. While reading Thomas Mann's "Tonio Kröger" and Franz Kafka's "The Judgement," one immediately notices contrasts in the authors' styles. Mann displays a highly detailed and descriptive style. His characters as well as their ideas are intricately drawn. Mann presents a full story, one that covers much of a lifetime, with an established plot that conveys a theme. On the other hand, Kafka develops his characters vaguely; his descriptions and statements frequently negate each other. Furthermore, this author presents more of a day-in-the-life story, in which little background is given. Ultimately, Kafka leaves the meaning of the story open to the reader's interpretation.

5.   People have discovered that visualization is an important ingredient to success. Used by athletes, visualization imprints success on the mind before the actual competition, thus building confidence that a winning performance is possible. Businesspeople have adopted this technique to overcome all sorts of obstacles because, to some, presenting a proposal at a meeting is as difficult as winning the Olympic diving competition. Furthermore, for both the athlete and the businessperson, visualization is the mental exercise necessary for peak performance.

6.   After World War II, Jacques-Yves Cousteau's attention turned to research on devices for underwater exploration. In 1943, with Emile Gagman, Cousteau received great acclaim for his invention of an underwater breathing apparatus, the Aqualung. The Aqualung, which allows divers to spend prolonged periods of time underwater, is used widely in exploration, in salvage operations, and in nautical archaeology, as well as in recreational diving. Later, in 1959, with Jean Mollard, Cousteau invented the Diving Saucer, a highly maneuverable submarine in which several observers can film the ocean's depth. Finally, in the early 1980s, Cousteau (along with his research team) added the Maulian Vent, a wind-powered ship with no sails, to his credits.

7.   In this chapter, we will follow, step by step, the process of developing a solution to a problem suitable for submitting to a computer. The problem we've chosen is very general: computing an average. We'll begin by carefully defining the problem to be solved. Next, we'll structure a human-level solution, using such generally accepted and understood everyday tools as a pocket calculator and a counter. Having specified a fairly complete human-level solution, we'll briefly discuss a few elementary computer concepts and restructure our solution to fit the requirements of these machines, developing a flowchart and the description of the data to be processed. Once we've completed these tasks, we'll be ready to begin coding the program in BASIC.

8.   On the other hand, this same technology that provides an information and entertainment boon to the home viewer presents an ongoing problem for the producers and copyright owners. Questions arise. How will copyright owners be reimbursed for providing free programs? Is our existing copyright law obsolete since the private viewer has the ability to take information that was meant to be shown only once? The old solutions to copyright infringement don't seem to apply.

Pulling It Together

A paragraph that is *planned*—that presents only one topic and then provides details to support that topic—is on the right track. Still, it may not be the best it can be. Transition, or pointer words, can make a paragraph more interesting and certainly clearer. *Transition words* or *phrases* tie the sentences together and help the reader follow the writer's line of thought.

Here is a paragraph with transition words in italics. What do the words do for you, the reader?

> Dear Mr. Ang:
> We know from your initial report that there is a strong market for widgets in the Northeast. *Now* the CEO and I would like you to begin a feasibility study. *In fact*, we will wait for the study before we talk to our banks about possible loans. *Moreover*, since manufacturing this new product would require additional staff, we'll need as much as six months to interview and hire candidates.

As you can see, transition words are not merely thrown into a paragraph. They're placed where they can contribute to the paragraph's meaning, and smooth the reader's way from the beginning of the paragraph to the end. In this paragraph, the word *now* switches the reader from the past (the initial report) to the present (the feasibility study). Then the words *in fact* emphasize that until Mr. Ang does his job the company cannot proceed with its plans. Finally, the word *moreover* introduces another reason why the company cannot begin manufacturing widgets for some time.

The more you read—both fiction and nonfiction—the more you'll realize that transition words fall into categories:

Time:	*now, later, before, after, last, while, then, first, second, finally, meanwhile, formerly*
Emphasis:	*indeed, in fact, certainly, clearly*
Contrast:	*yet, however, but, although, whereas, nonetheless, on the contrary, on the other hand, nevertheless*
Similarity:	*similarly, just as, likewise, in the same way*
Illustration:	*for example, for instance, to illustrate, in this way, specifically*
Conclusion:	*therefore, consequently, in other words, in conclusion*
Addition:	*moreover, in addition, besides, too, also, furthermore*

PRACTICE 4

1. Insert the words *nonetheless, indeed,* and *meanwhile* where they belong in the following paragraph:

Dear Ms. Baum:

Please forgive us: We've just discovered that our computer has been spewing out duplicate bills. _____, we've found that you paid your bill within ten days of receiving it. We hope, _____, that you will remain a friend. _____ you are a valued customer.

2. Insert the words *on the contrary* and *furthermore* where they belong in the following paragraph:

I really don't think it is fair to blame this decline of eloquence entirely on the general public. As the entertainment industry has grown into its presently mammoth proportions, the distractions available to the common person, from movies to music to the opera, have quietly pushed ceremonial orations, political debates, and general knowledge lectures off the podium. Instead of using this mass communication marvel to make important statements, the "minds" of Hollywood produce "mindless rot," which the masses kindly consume and then ask for more.

3. Insert the words *finally, first,* and *then* where they belong in the following paragraph:

In his *Book of Lists,* Irving Wallace ranks fear of public speaking among the top ten fears, right after death by violence. You can beat that fear by being well prepared and by following this plan in your next presentation. Capture your audience's attention immediately with a question or a statement that pulls the listeners out of their own thoughts and onto your wavelength. State your position. Give your listeners a way to think, a viewpoint. Follow up with statistical charts, ideas in picture form, or visual aids that tell your story. If you want your listeners to do something, leave them with something to do: a sample letter to their state representatives (with addresses), a ready-to-mail order form, a request for information to your company.

PRACTICE 5

In the following paragraphs, insert transition words to clarify and tie together the ideas. Choose words from the list on page 00.

1. At the office, guard against setting up unrealistic schedules. Don't create false deadlines, or you will set yourself up for stress at the same time. You may be eager to finish a project quickly. Don't tell your boss or your customer that the job will be done in an absurdly short time. That won't

help. You may slow down your working time by creating an unnecessary time limit.

2.   The cellular phone industry is working on safer ways for people to dial from car telephones. Hands-free systems allow drivers to look straight ahead while talking. They still have to look away to dial. One car manufacturer offers a phone on the visor. The driver's eyes remain closer to the road in front. Another manufacturer is about to place a touch screen dialer with large numbers near the steering wheel. Drivers will still have to look away for a second or two until voice-activated dialing is developed.

3.   Nutritional information on food labels has been overhauled. The Food and Drug Administration requires the addition of information about disease-causing substances. Those food elements are cholesterol, saturated fat, and calories from fat. Other food components—thiamine, riboflavin, niacin and one protein—have been dropped because they are no longer linked to health problems in the United States. Products that call themselves cholesterol free have to contain less than 20 milligrams of cholesterol per serving with less than 5 grams of total fat and less than 2 grams of saturated fat per serving.

4.   Did you know that the words "ALL NATURAL" on a label do not mean that the food is, necessarily, a better product? It does mean that the food contains no additives or preservatives. Consider that an additive such as ascorbic acid raises the nutrient level (vitamin C) in fruit products as well as helping the fruit to keep its color. Other additives keep foods fresh in both taste and texture. Obviously, "ALL NATURAL" is not always "ALL the BETTER."

5.   At a job interview, expect to be asked questions especially designed to test your competence in that particular job. The interviewer undoubtedly will ask questions that check your knowledge of the special words, or jargon, connected with the job. The interviewer may want to know how effective a problem solver you are. Be ready for an informal problem-solving test in which you review, discuss, and decide on a solution to a problem. You may have to perform an actual job task—use a machine, type a letter, do some laboratory procedure—and finish it correctly in a reasonable amount of time.

ANSWERS

PRACTICE 1

Answers may vary.

1. Computers have changed how fighter planes fly; they've also changed the demands we make on pilots.
2. Writing a business plan will help the company examine its present status and its plans for the future.

PRACTICE 2

1. Reproduction, of course, is the key to an organism's survival.
2. We predict that our company will soon be able to link up your home or office with the worldwide information explosion.
3. Used in the following way, a card system will keep your notes organized and prevent your retracting steps.
4. This year we need to assess the impact an aging population will have on our business.
5. This geography, harsh climate, different languages, and divergent cultures often make that land seem less like a single nation and more like a conservative collection of feuding fiefdoms.
6. Successful business trainers say that the most important component of a business letter is its friendly tone.
7. Take the advice of the Social Security Administration and periodically check the agency's record of your earnings.

PRACTICE 3

1. Plan: Gives details that explain the topic sentence.
2. Plan: Defends the opinion stated in the topic sentence.
3. Plan: Explains a process.
4. Plan: Gives examples that contrast the work of two authors.
5. Plan: Explains a process stated in the topic sentence.
6. Plan: Describes chronologically what the topic sentence states.
7. Plan: Defines (or explains) a process.
8. Plan: Links the topic sentence to an earlier topic.

PRACTICE 4

1. Dear Ms. Baum:
   Please forgive us! We've just discovered that our computer has been spewing out duplicate bills. *Meanwhile*, we've found that you paid your bill within ten days of receiving it. We hope, *nonetheless*, that you will remain a friend. *Indeed*, you are a valued customer.
2. I really don't think it is fair to blame this decline of eloquence entirely on the general public. *On the contrary*, as the entertainment industry has grown into its presently mammoth proportions, the distractions available to the common person from movies to music to the opera have quietly pushed ceremonial orations, political debates, and general knowledge lectures off the podium. *Furthermore*, instead of using this mass communication marvel to make important statements, the "minds" of Hollywood produce "mindless rot," which the masses kindly consume and then ask for more.
3. In his *Book of Lists*, Irving Wallace ranks fear of public speaking among the top ten fears, right after death by violence. You can beat that fear by being well prepared and by following this plan in your next presentation. *First*, capture your audience's attention immediately with a question or statement that pulls

the listeners out of their own thoughts and onto your wavelength. *Then*, state your position. Give your listeners a way to think, a viewpoint. Follow up with statistical charts, ideas in picture form, or visual aids that tell your story. *Finally*, if you want your listeners to do something, leave them with something to do: a sample letter to their state representatives (with addresses), a ready-to-mail order form, a request for information to your company.

PRACTICE 5

1. At the office, guard against setting up unrealistic schedules. For example, don't create false deadlines or you will set yourself up for stress at the same time. Although you may be eager to finish a project quickly, don't tell your boss or your customer that the job will be done in an absurdly short time. That won't help. *On the contrary,* you may slow down your working time by creating an unnecessary time limit.

2. The cellular phone industry is working on safer ways for people to dial from car telephones. Although hands-free systems allow drivers to look straight ahead while talking, they still have to look away to dial. One car manufacturer, for example, offers a phone on the visor so that the driver's eyes remain closer to the road in front. Similarly, another manufacturer is about to place a touch-screen dialer with large numbers near the steering wheel. *Nonetheless,* drivers will still have to look away for a second or two until voice-activated dialing is developed.

3. Nutritional information on food labels has been overhauled. First, the Food and Drug Administration requires the addition of information about disease-causing substances, *specifically* cholesterol, saturated fat, and calories from fat. *Second,* other food components—thiamine, riboflavin, niacin, and one protein—have been dropped because they are no longer linked to health problems in the United States. *Finally,* products that call themselves cholesterol free have to contain less than 20 milligrams of cholesterol per serving with less than 5 grams of total fat and less than 2 grams of saturated fat per serving.

4. Did you know that the words "ALL NATURAL" on a label do *not* mean that the food is, necessarily, a better product? *On the other hand,* it does mean that the food contains no additives or preservatives. *However,* consider that an additive such as ascorbic acid raises the nutrient level (vitamin C) in fruit products as well as helping the fruit to keep its color. *In the same way,* other additives keep foods fresh in both taste and texture. Obviously, "ALL NATURAL" is not always "ALL the BETTER."

5. At a job interview, expect to be asked questions especially designed to test your competence in that particular job. *For example,* the interviewer undoubtedly will ask questions that check your knowledge of the special words, or jargon, connected with the job. *Moreover,* the interviewer may want to know how effective a problem solver you are. *Consequently,* be ready for an informal problem-solving test in which you review, discuss, and decide on a solution to a problem. *And, finally,* you may have to perform an actual job task—use a machine, type a letter, do some laboratory procedure—and finish it correctly in a reasonable amount of time.

6.

Write Strong Sentences

In solving many of the word problems in your business report, letter, or term paper, you have probably made your written work a good deal more readable. Now you need to look at your sentences and make some important improvements in style.

Important Ideas

Each sentence you write should attract your reader's interest by being *emphatic*—that is, by clearly stressing the most important idea in the sentence. You can usually achieve emphasis by placing the key idea at the end of the sentence.

Take a look, for instance, at part of a report on revitalizing city property. This section of the report emphasizes the tenants' role. The example below shows one of the sentences written in two different ways. Which sentence do you think does a better job?

1. The tenant activists who conceived of the idea make the rebirth of this housing unique.
2. The rebirth of this housing is unique because it was the tenant activists who conceived of the idea.

Sentence 2 gives the reader a clearer picture of the active role the tenants played in the rehabilitation project.

Look at another example from the report that points out the far-reaching results of this project.

1. The way the project was rehabilitated, particularly the reduction in the number of apartments per building, will help set the standards for future public housing.
2. The way the project was rehabilitated will help set the standard for future public housing, particularly because of the reduction in the number of apartments per building.

Which sentence leaves you with the idea that the project will have a far-reaching effect? Sentence 1 does the better job.

PRACTICE 1

Rewrite the following sentences. Put the more important idea at the end of each sentence.

1. Clear understanding of the company's goals is the chief aim of our new manual.

2. Investors listen when that brokerage house talks.

3. It is hard enough to prepare for today, let alone for the future, in our confusing economic climate.

4. The company could be entering a period of sustained growth if current trends continue.

5. Before supplies run out, the assistant manager should replace them.

6. You should file a report if you have an accident.

7. Before the banks close make out the checks.

8. Place original signatures on all three copies after you have read the additional clauses.

9. The census has provided a picture of who we are and how we live since 1790.

10. Key terms are cross-referenced, just as in an index.

Unnecessary Words

You may think that there are no more unnecessary words in your report, letter, or memo. Look again. You can still pare away lengthy clauses and replace them with phrases or even with single words.

No:	*Because there were updrafts,* the flight was bumpy.
Yes:	*Updrafts* made the flight bumpy.

No:	*So that we can meet our production schedule,* we'll need new equipment by the 15th.
Yes:	*To meet* our production schedule, we'll need new equipment by the 15th.

No:	Order paper *that is suitable for our new word processor.*
Yes:	Order *suitable* (or the *right*) paper for our new word processor.

PRACTICE 2

Trim away any unnecessary words in these sentences.

1. We were searching for a salesperson who had experience.

2. Here is a sample of our new design, which we have just introduced.

3. On the wall there were a great many signs that had been made by hand.

4. The farmers here raise blueberries, which are purchased mainly for frozen pies.

5. At one time, the deficit was the most serious problem that was affecting business in the United States.

6. At this point in time, we have not as yet made a decision on your promotion.

7. In 1943–1947 is when Clare Booth Luce served in the House of Representatives.

8. Once the group had been dispersed, traffic was able to flow.

9. Unfortunately, the furniture is too large in size.

10. We are thinking in terms of hiring more staff.

Action Words

Simplify your sentences by using an action word instead of a more roundabout group of words. In the following example, the second sentence is simpler, more effective. Notice that the verb *has decided* takes the place of a wordy verb-and-noun group.

No: The committee *has reached a decision* to hire you for the position.
Yes: The committee *has decided* to hire you for the position.

Look at another example. Here again an action word replaces a verb and noun.

No: This insurance program *makes a distinction* between new and old employees.
Yes: This insurance program *distinguishes* between new and old employees.

PRACTICE 3

Simplify these sentences.

1. The government finally made a suggestion that we delay the retirement age.
2. You can conserve energy if you have knowledge of the sources of waste.
3. Before you send your final recommendation, make a draft proposal.
4. Our representative sent an invitation to their ambassador.
5. The two countries reached an agreement to end the boycott.
6. The teacher agreed that he would make an adjustment in my grade.
7. If Thomas still raises an objection to the conference date, we will change it.
8. We will do an inspection of the product just before it is shipped.
9. The inhabitants of Low Torning furnished an explanation to the hero of the book.
10. Today, the union expects to reach an end in its debate over benefits.

Active and Passive

Whenever you can, use active verbs instead of passive ones. Active verbs usually make the meaning more accessible because they sound immediate. They occur in a *subject-verb-object* pattern. This sentence pattern quickly answers the question "Who does what?" For example:

Subject	*Active* Verb		*Direct* Object
↓	↓		↓

The company offers a comprehensive medical plan.

Who? The company. Action? Offer. What? A plan. In addition, when active verbs replace passive verbs, shorter and more forceful sentences result. In many cases, using an active verb changes the subject's placement—for the better.

Passive: The management team was *hired* by the company.
Active: The company *hired* a management team.
Note: The word *was* makes the sentence passive.

Passive: For novices in office management, a special seminar *is needed*.
Active: Novices in office management *need* a special seminar.
Note: The word *is* makes the sentence passive.

In each case the "lost" or buried subject takes its rightful place in the sentence when the active verb is used.

A passive verb, on the other hand, turns the thought around, as in the following:

Passive
Subject   Verb
  ↓   ↓
A comprehensive medical plan *is offered* by the company.

In this sentence the subject does not act; the subject is acted upon. The reader has to get to the end of the sentence to find out who did the offering.

Generally, then, when an active verb replaces a passive verb, a more straightforward sentence results. Readers move from subject to action to object, getting the meaning as they read along the line of print. Although the passive pattern is technically correct, the action pattern is more straightforward.

Does this mean that you must never use passive verbs? Not at all. Occasionally you may want to shift the emphasis of a sentence from who *performed* the action to who *received* the action. For example:

The management team *was credited* by the board with hiring a successful marketing manager.

In this case, the writer placed *the management team* in the subject position for emphasis. Who gave the team the credit is not especially important.

On other occasions, you may not want an "actor," or "doers," in the subject of your sentence. If, for example, you want to report a happening but don't want to reveal who did it, use the passive. For example:

A work stoppage *is expected* on Tuesday.

The writer does not want to reveal (or doesn't know) who expects a work stoppage. Another example:

A decision to close three of the five departments *was made* at the board meeting.

Again, the writer does not want to say (or doesn't know) who made the decision.

The passive sentence pattern is often used in scientific writing, because it provides the objective stance that science writers prefer. (In scientific writing, personal references, such as *I, you, or we*, almost never appear.) Here is how one science writer used the passive voice:

A physical model *is* often *used* by chemists to understand the behavior of matter.

In this sentence, the subject (*model*) does not perform the action. Instead, it is acted upon (*is used*). Although the sentence mentions who performed the action—*chemists*—the writer considers the action—use of the models—more important than the "doer" or "actor."

Here are two more examples:

A theory *is retained* only so long as it is useful to scientists.
Some kinds of matter *are* easily *observed* by scientists.

A final note: The passive sentence pattern does have a place in nonscientific writing. However, when writers use it continually, eliminating the *actor-action* pattern from their writing, their letters, memos, and reports become stilted and vague.

PRACTICE 4

In the following sentences, change passive verbs to active ones. (Using an active verb will help you find the "lost" or buried subject. For example, in the first sentence, change "cannot be allowed" to "cannot allow." Ask yourself, "Who cannot allow?" The answer reveals the subject of the sentence.)

1   A partial credit on your order *cannot be allowed* by us.
2. Hundreds of these letters *are received* by people.
3. The material you sent us *was inspected* by us.
4. He *was called* a traitor by Napoleon.
5. It *is believed* that an additional person in the South will complete our sales group.
6. In the book, a treatment designed to pressure Stanley into conforming *is proposed* by his doctor.
7. Despite the talk of economies and cutbacks, a profit *was* not *realized* by the company.
8. This decision to offer flexible benefits *was initiated* by the Human Resources Department.
9. Logging-in *can be accomplished* only after you hear the high beep.
10. It *has been decided* that we will join the computer update service.

Balanced Sentences

When you write, make your ideas as easy as possible to follow. One way to provide smooth sailing for your readers is to write balanced sentences. In a *balanced sentence*, each item in a series of related actions, descriptions, or ideas is expressed in the same grammatical form. The following sentence, for example, is not balanced:

Executives rank *business writing, office politics,* and *being delayed in airports* as their chief annoyances.

There are three items in this series: *business writing, office politics,* and *being delayed in airports.* You probably noticed, though, that the third item sounds wrong, because it's in a different form from the other two items.

The challenge is to make the third item match the first two. Change *being delayed* to a descriptive word and a noun: *airport delays.* Now the sentence is balanced:

Executives rank *business writing, office politics,* and *airport delays* as their chief annoyances.

Here's another sentence that lacks balance:

Robert Todd Lincoln *practiced law* in Chicago, *became president* of the Pullman Company, and *he was a director* of various banks.

Here, too, there are three items in a series. Which one is in a different form from the others? Again it is the last one: *he was a director.* To correct this error, change this word group to an action verb:

Robert Todd Lincoln *practiced law* in Chicago, *became president* of the Pullman Company, and *directed various banks.*

PRACTICE 5

Rewrite each sentence so that related ideas are expressed in the same form.

1. Write your evaluation truthfully and record your comments in a concise way.
2. The housing project is a benefit to the neighborhood, and it will be a credit to the sponsors.
3. The attainment of freedom and achieving national security were their goals.
4. Many people in the wealthiest nation in the world are destitute, malnourished, and don't have jobs.
5. This new machine is neither faster nor does it work more quietly.
6. Harriet plans the in-service programs, hires the staff, and is the manager of the office as well.

7. XYZ Corporation promises to service our machines, to keep needed parts in stock, and they will charge us reasonable prices.

8. To find a job, read newspaper advertisements, ask your friends for leads, and there are employment agencies you can call.

9. Our resources were gradually depleted as settlers moved across the country, built homes and industry, and then they failed to renew what they used.

10. Before you sign a contract, read it carefully, and then you can ask your lawyer to check it.

Related Ideas

Your sentences should be simple, correct, and natural sounding. But that doesn't mean they all have to be short. As you read the following paragraph, think about how it sounds.

> A flowchart serves as a reference document. It describes the logical flow of a program. And it's in an easy-to-follow form. Most programs will change over time. This is particularly true of business programs. Documentation is essential. The flowchart is a valuable tool.

The paragraph sounds stilted—and for good reasons. The sentences offer almost no variety. They are all around the same length (seven or eight words). Reading them is about as exciting as listening to a clock tick. Also, there is no sense of what is most important or least important, because every thought receives the same emphasis. Although the individual sentences may be easy to read, they are misleading because the relationships between sentences are not explained. Only by combining ideas, by making some ideas less important and others more important, can you put some variety, interest, and focus into the paragraph.

One caution! Avoid relying on the word *and* when you combine related thoughts. *And* is useful sometimes, but it doesn't always show the precise relationship between two ideas. For example:

> A flowchart tells what must be done and a flowchart defines the order in which the steps must be performed.

The sentence gives equal emphasis to the two ideas joined by *and*. In fact, the writer meant to say something like this:

> We've already said that a flowchart tells what must be done. Now add to your information that a flowchart defines the order in which these steps must be performed.

Or the writer might simply say:

> In *addition* to telling what must be done, a flowchart defines the order in which the steps must be performed.

Certain words and phrases help you express the relationships that sentences and sentence parts have to each other. For example, by using the word *that,* you can establish the relationship between the first and second sentences of the paragraph given above.

> A flowchart serves as a reference document *that* describes the logical flow of the program.

Here's a hint. Whenever you find that you've written a sentence beginning with *it is* (or *it's*) or *there are,* see if you can establish a relationship between that sentence and the one before it.

Let's go on to the third sentence in the paragraph above. The word *and* indicates that an idea in this sentence is linked to an idea in the preceding sentence. Moreover, this third sentence contains the word *it's.* Apply the hint given above, and your sentence becomes:

> A flowchart serves as a reference document *that* describes the logical flow of a program in an easy-to-follow form.

A similar opportunity exists in the next few sentences. You can tie together sentences 4 and 5 easily. Two words in sentence 5—*This is*—are clues to the fact that the sentences are begging to be joined, because this refers to the idea expressed in sentence 4. Furthermore, *most programs* in sentence 4 and *business programs* in sentence 5 are related. Put them together:

> Most programs, particularly business programs, will change over time.

How does *Documentation is essential* relate to the preceding sentences? Simple. Since programs change over time, the changes must be documented as they occur. In this case, *since* is the combining word. If you rethink your newest sentence:

> Most programs, particularly business programs, will change over time

to include the word *since,* you can include the fact that documentation is essential:

> Since most programs, particularly business programs, will change over time, documentation is essential.

As a reference document, the flowchart is a valuable tool. What word could you add to the final sentence to show its relationship to the paragraph? Try this:

> Since most programs, particularly business programs, will change over time, documentation is essential. *Consequently,* the flowchart is a valuable documentation tool.

Now compare the revised paragraph with the original, choppy paragraph on page 98:

> A flowchart serves as a reference document that describes the logical flow of a program in an easy-to-follow form. Since most programs, particularly business programs, will change over time, documentation is essential. Consequently, the flowchart is a valuable documentation tool.

Subordinating Words

A group of words, including *since, although*, and *if,* are especially useful in combining ideas. These words are called *subordinating words* because they show that one idea in a sentence is less important than—or subordinant to—another idea in the sentence. Moreover, subordinating words add information and lend variety to a communication as a whole. A list of some of these words follows.

after	if	when
although	since	where
as	though	whereas
because	unless	

To understand how subordinating words can be used to stress one idea over another, look at the following two sentences.

> We have rented all the offices. We expect the building to show a profit this year.

The writer decided to combine the two sentences to emphasize the fact that now the building would show a profit. The subordinating word *since* makes *We have rented all the offices* less important than the rest of the sentence:

> *Since* we have rented all the offices, we expect the building to show a profit this year.

PRACTICE 6

In each item below, use the information to write a sentence in which one idea is more important than the other. Use a word from the list above to subordinate one idea to the other.

1. Give me all the data by January 15. The report won't be in on time.
2. We will arrive. We expect the meeting room to be ready.
3. We requested the parts three weeks ago. The parts have not arrived yet.
4. We worked hard. Our department has succeeded.
5. He programmed the computer. He had figured out which project would suit our needs.
6. The transformer arrived. The machine worked.
7. There's smoke. There's fire.
8. Our paperwork was on time and our project was completed. We still didn't receive a commendation.
9. You do the typing. I'll come in early to polish the report.
10. Hunger can keep people awake. Dieters should reserve a few calories for a bedtime snack.

Connecting Words

Another group of words plays an important role in combining ideas—the *connecting words*. Two lists of connecting words follow. The first contains words that combine ideas or sentences that the writer considers to be equal in importance. The words in the second group also link equal ideas, but these coordinating words are used in pairs.

Words That Link Coordinate Sentences or Ideas of Equal Importance:

and	accordingly
but	also
for	besides
nor	consequently
or	further, furthermore
so	however
yet	moreover
	then
	therefore
	thus

Words Used in Pairs to Relate One Sentence Element to Another:

both—and
either—or
neither—nor
not only—but also
whether—or

The following examples show how you can use connecting words to combine sentences:

Separate: When you write an essay exam, jot down a few notes first. Use numbers to put the notes in proper sequence.

Combined: When you write an essay exam, jot down a few notes first; *then* use numbers to put the notes in proper sequence.

Separate: The police officers could not explain the cause of the accident. They could not locate a witness.

Combined: The police officers could not explain the cause of the accident, *nor* could they locate a witness.

Separate: Several employees have expressed an interest in a company child-care center. The personnel manager will investigate the possibility.

Combined: Several employees have expressed an interest in a company child-care center; *accordingly*, the personnel manager will investigate the possibility.

Separate: Style guides discuss the steps in researching your subject. They also discuss the steps in footnoting your sources.

Combined: Style guides discuss the steps *not only* in researching your subject *but also* in footnoting your sources.

(*Not only* and *but also* are both followed by prepositional phrases. When you use pairs of connecting words, be sure that they are followed by words or word groups that are like in form.)

Separate: The office manager filled the space with furniture that was not attractive. The furniture was not useful, either.

Combined: The office manager filled the space with furniture that was *neither* attractive *nor* useful.

In combining related thoughts, bear in mind that *and* may not show the exact relationship between two ideas. For example:

The questionnaire revealed that not all employees needed or wanted the same benefits, *and* the company decided to offer three different packages.

The sentence gives equal emphasis to the two ideas joined by *and.* In fact, the writer meant to say that the second part of the sentence was *a result* of the first part. A connecting word like *therefore* in front of the second idea would have made the point clearer:

The questionnaire revealed that not all employees needed or wanted the same benefits; *therefore,* the company decided to offer three different packages.

Notice that a semicolon comes before a connector like *therefore, however,* or *consequently* when it takes the place of *and* in a sentence. A comma usually comes after the connecting word.

PRACTICE 7

In each of the following items, combine the two sentences by using one of the connecting words from the list on page 101.

1. Orientation sets the stage for training. It smoothes the way for what is to come.

2. Transfers require planning. So do promotions.

3. We want you to have widgets for $1.49 each. We can offer the reduced price for two weeks only.

4. We hope that the new program will attract qualified applicants from among our employees. We are publicizing it in the company newsletter.

5. The prospectus didn't say how long the project would take. It didn't include an application form.

6. No amount of debate reassured the community about the landfill. They did not want the incinerator either.

7. They lobbied the town government for a year. They finally convinced city officials that recycling would get rid of 60 percent of the garbage.

8. When the committee considered Jason for the promotion, they decided he was not effective in leading all the departments. He also was not a model of cooperation.

9. If you do that, we can't achieve our goal. I have to override your decision.

10. You can drive to Attleboro. After that, you can take a train to Boston.

PRACTICE 8

Sentences

This exercise will help you review what you have learned about writing strong sentences. Rewrite the following sentences to improve their style.

1. The end of a sentence is the place where the interesting information should be.

2. In the past, recession, high interest rates, and competing with foreign auto markets hit manufacturers hard.

3. Once the meeting has been concluded, return to work.

4. I want to make a proposal in favor of a four-day work week.

5. The manual is printed by our Production Department.

6. Workers still expect leadership from their supervisors. And they expect them to be impartial in exercising it.

7. The supervisors thought employees had more interest in job security. Also the employees put more emphasis on satisfaction from the work itself.

8. Give the computer a program. You can instruct the computer to execute the logic over and over again.

9. Seward couldn't get congressional approval to purchase islands in the Caribbean Sea. He did get consent to buy Alaska from Russia.

10. The skeleton is a rigid or semirigid structure that provides support for animals' soft tissues. It provides leverage for muscular action.

PRACTICE 9

Paragraphs

In the following paragraphs, apply what you have learned about writing strong sentences. Rewrite as many of the sentences as necessary to improve their style.

The United States, too, had its own theory on which it based its expansion during the mid-eighteenth century. It was called Manifest Destiny. "A future event accepted as inevitable" is what Manifest Destiny literally means. During the Polk era of the 1840s, Manifest Destiny was the belief that the American future was to live in and possess North America. And that the country would be a place of freedom of religion, democracy, and republicanism.

The actual percentage of believers in Manifest Destiny at the time of Polk's election is not known. Polk's views on expansion definitely were the reason he was elected. The Democrats were the chief advocates of Manifest Destiny. The ideology was spread by Democratic papers all along the North Atlantic seacoast, where expansionists were loud in their advocacy of it.

ANSWERS

PRACTICE 1
1. The chief aim of our new manual is a clear understanding of the company's goals.
2. When that brokerage house talks, investors listen.
3. In our confusing economic climate, it is hard enough to prepare for today, let alone for the future.
4. If current trends continue, the company could be entering a period of sustained growth.
5. The assistant manager should replace supplies before they run out.
6. If you have an accident, file a report.
7. Make out the checks before the banks close.
8. After you have read the additional clauses, place original signatures on all three copies.
9. Since 1790, the census has provided a picture of who we are and how we live.
10. Just as in an index, key terms are cross-referenced.

PRACTICE 2
1. We were searching for an experienced salesperson.
2. Here is a sample of our newly introduced design.
3. A great many handmade signs were on the wall.
4. The farmers here raise blueberries mainly for frozen pies.
5. At one time, the deficit was the most serious problem affecting business in the United States.
6. We have not yet decided on your promotion.
7. In 1943–1947, Clare Boothe Luce served in the House of Representatives.
8. Once the group had been dispersed, traffic flowed.
9. Unfortunately, the furniture is too large.
10. We are thinking of hiring more staff.

PRACTICE 3
1. The government finally suggested that we delay the retirement age.
2. You can conserve energy if you know the sources of waste.
3. Before you send your final recommendation, draft a proposal.
4. Our representative invited their ambassador.
5. The two countries agreed to end the boycott.
6. The teacher agreed to adjust my grade.
7. If Thomas still objects to the conference date, we will change it.
8. We will inspect the product just before it is shipped.
9. The inhabitants of Low Torning explained to the book's hero.
10. Today, the union expects to conclude its debate over benefits.

PRACTICE 4
1. We *cannot allow* a partial credit on your order.
2. People *receive* hundreds of these letters.
3. We *inspected* the material you sent us.
4. Napoleon *called* him a traitor.
5. We *believe* that an additional person in the South will complete our sales group.
6. In the book, Stanley's doctor *proposes* a treatment designed to pressure him into conforming.

7. Despite the talk of economies and cutbacks, the company *did* not *realize* a profit.
8. The Human Resources Department *initiated* this decision to offer flexible benefits.
9. You *can* log in only after you hear the high beep.
10. We *have decided* to join the computer update service.

PRACTICE 5
1. Write your evaluation truthfully and record your comments *concisely.*
2. The housing project is a benefit to the neighborhood and a *credit to the sponsors.*
3. *Attaining* freedom and achieving national security were their goals.
    or
    The attainment of freedom and the achievement of national security were their goals.
4. Many people in the wealthiest nation in the world are destitute, malnourished, and *jobless.*
5. This new machine is neither faster nor *quieter.*
6. Harriet plans the in-service programs, hires the staff, and *manages the office as well.*
7. XYZ Corporation promises to service our machines, to keep needed parts in stock, and *to charge us reasonable prices.*
8. To find a job, read newspaper advertisements, ask your friends for leads, and *call employment agencies.*
9. Our resources were gradually depleted as settlers moved across the country, built homes and industry, and *failed to renew what they used.*
10. Before you sign a contract, read it carefully and *ask your lawyer to check it.*

PRACTICE 6
1. Unless you give me all the data by January 15, the report won't be in on time.
2. When we arrive, we expect the meeting room to be ready.
3. Although we requested the parts three weeks ago, they have not arrived yet.
4. Because we worked hard, our department has succeeded.
5. He programmed the computer after he had figured out which project would suit our needs.
6. After the transformer arrived, the machine worked.
7. Where there's smoke there's fire.
8. Though our paperwork was on time and our project was completed, we didn't receive a commendation.
9. If you do the typing, I'll come in early to polish the report.
10. Because hunger can keep people awake, dieters should reserve a few calories for a bedtime snack.

PRACTICE 7
1. Orientation not only sets the stage for training but also smooths the way for what is to come.
2. Both transfers and promotions require planning.
3. We want you to have the widgets for $1.49 each; however, we can offer this reduced price for two weeks only.
4. We hope that the new program will attract qualified applicants from among our employees; therefore (*or* consequently *or* accordingly), we are publicizing it in the company newsletter.
5. The prospectus didn't say how long the project would take, nor did it include an application form.
6. No amount of debate reassured the community about the landfill or the incinerator.
7. They lobbied their town government for a year and finally convinced city officials that recycling would get rid of 60 percent of the garbage.
8. When the committee considered Jason for the promotion, they decided he was neither effective in leading all the departments nor a model of cooperation.

9. If you do that, we can't achieve our goal; consequently, I have to override your decision.
10. You can drive to Attleboro, then take a train to Boston.

PRACTICE 8

Answers may vary.
1. The interesting information should be at the end of a sentence.
2. In the past, recession, high interest rates, and competition with foreign auto markets hit manufacturers hard.
3. After the meeting, return to work.
4. I propose a four-day work week.
5. Our Production Department prints the manual.
6. While workers still expect leadership from their supervisors, they expect them to be impartial in exercising it.
7. Although the supervisors thought employees were more interested in job security, the employees put more emphasis on job satisfaction.
8. After you program a computer, you can instruct it to execute the logic over and over again.
9. Although Seward couldn't get congressional approval to purchase islands in the Caribbean Sea, he did get consent to buy Alaska from Russia.
10. The skeleton is a rigid or semirigid structure supporting animals' soft tissues and providing leverage for muscular action.

PRACTICE 9

Answers may vary.
   During the mid-eighteenth century, the United States based its expansion upon the theory of Manifest Destiny. Manifest Destiny literally means "a future event accepted as inevitable." During the Polk era of the 1840s, the theory held that the American future was to live in and possess North America, where the people would enjoy freedom of religion, democracy, and republicanism.
   We do not know the actual percentage of people who believed in Manifest Destiny at the time of Polk's election. We do know, however, that Polk's views on expansion were instrumental in his election. In fact, as chief advocates of Manifest Destiny, the Democrats spread the ideology all along the North Atlantic seacoast with the help of expansionists, who were loud in their advocacy.

7.

Survive Grammar

Eliza Doolittle was "labeled" by her Cockney accent. Simple grammar errors can destroy your image, too. Sometimes, because "everyone" misuses a word or phrase, we assume the misuse is appropriate. It may be acceptable between friends in conversation, but not on paper, in school, or at the office.

The following paragraph includes several common errors. Can you spot them? Can you correct them?

> Everyone, in their own way, make the best of a difficult situation. For example, my boss and me were having lunch at a popular restaurant. Suddenly, a person who neither of us knew came to our table. He pretended that he knew my boss and I very well and asked to join us for lunch. We tried to say no, but he sat right down. As things turned out, he was very interesting company. Me and my boss had to leave suddenly. Because we had a meeting. We thanked him for lunch and left.

Did you find the errors? Read the corrected paragraph.

> Everyone, in *his* own way, *makes* the best of a difficult situation. For example, my boss and *I* were having lunch at a popular restaurant. Suddenly, a person *whom* neither of us knew came to our table. He pretended that he knew my boss and *me* very well and asked to join us for lunch. We tried to say no, but he sat right down. As things turned out, he was very interesting company. *My boss and I* had to leave *suddenly because* we had a meeting. We thanked him for lunch and left.

Lack of agreement of subject and verb, misplaced modifiers, sentence fragments, and misuse of pronouns are common errors.

Agreement Between Subject and Verb

Subject-verb agreement means using a singular verb with a singular noun and a plural verb with a plural noun. This sounds simple. It can, however, be confusing because nouns and verbs do not follow the same rules when changing from singular to plural.

The rules will also be different depending on the sentence pattern. Do you remember the two basic sentence patterns you read about in the section titled "Active and Passive" in Chapter 6? For the early part of this chapter, we will only be working with active voice sentences. An active sentence follows the pattern: subject-verb-object. In the sentence below, company is the subject, offers is the verb, and medical plan is the object.

> Example: The company offers a comprehensive medical plan.

Look at the following active-voice sentence and think about which verb is correct.

Leon (use/uses) that program to edit his report.

1st	I	we
2nd	you	you
3rd	he, she, it, *Leon*	they

First, determine whether the subject is singular or plural and whether the subject is first (I), second (you), or third (he, she, it, or a single name) person. In this case, Leon is singular and third person.

If the subject is first or second person singular or any plural, the *s* is not added to the verb. If, for example, the subject of the sample sentence were in the third person plural, the *s* would not be added to the verb: *Our employees* (plural subject) *use* (plural active verb—no *s*) *that program to edit their reports.*

The *s* is only added to the end of the verb when third person singular is used. For example, Leon *uses* that program. Third person plural would *not* have an *s*: They *use* that program. This may seem contradictory because an *s* means plural on a subject word or other noun. This is not the case, however, with verbs. Added as a verb ending, the *s* means the verb is singular.

I use	we use
you use	you use
he, she, it, Leon uses	they use

PRACTICE 1

Complete the following paragraph, selecting the correct verb form to complete each sentence.

The subway platform is very crowded at 8 A.M. Tourists (rush, rushes) to get started early. Many of the businesspeople (attempt, attempts) to get to their offices before 9 A.M., and workers returning from the 12 A.M. shift also (crowd, crowds) the platform. One of the conductors (is, are) especially interesting to watch during this hectic time. He (shout, shouts) directions and (signal, signals) with his hands as though he were a performer in a Broadway show. Crowds of people (stop, stops) in their haste to observe this showman. One of the commuters (offer, offers) coffee to him each morning. Without skipping a beat, he (accept, accepts) it with a wink of thanks.

Special Case: Confusing Subjects

When it comes to determining whether the subject is singular or plural, some are more difficult to recognize. Words such as *everyone, each, any, everybody, somebody,* and *anybody* are singular and take a singular verb, even when referring to more than one (in the examples below, *them, staff, times*).

Each of them *enjoys* studying on our campus.
None of our staff *leaves* before 6 P.M.
None of the meeting times *is* acceptable.

Some can be used both in the singular and in the plural.

Somebody interrupts whenever I speak.
Some people always *interrupt.*

Words such as *all, few, several, both,* and *many* are plural.

Both of my briefcases are ruined.
Many of the dishes in this restaurant are spicy.
Several performers host parties after the show.
A *few* of the instructors have additional jobs.
All of the applicants were interviewed last Friday.

Special Case: Verb Placement

Some of the sentences in the previous section may seem confusing because the verb does not directly follow the subject. For example, there is no question that the following sentence is correct:

The applications arrive in the morning mail.

Applications is plural and *arrive* (without an *s*) is the plural verb form. The next sentence is clearly correct, too:

All of the applications arrive in the morning mail.

All is the subject of the sentence, not *applications.* If, however, we quickly read *applications arrive* as the subject and verb, we won't get into trouble. *All* is plural, too. Please note the following description:

	Descriptive	*Active*
Subject	*Phrase*	*Verb*
↓	↓	↓

All (of the applications) arrive in the morning mail.

Now note the following sentence:

One of the applications arrive in the morning mail.

By quickly misinterpreting "applications" as the subject, you can miss the error in the sentence. What is the subject? One. One *arrives.*

One (of the applications) *arrives* in the morning mail.

Special Case: Either . . . Or

Either…or takes a verb that agrees with the second choice.

Either the tree or the *bushes have* to go.
Either the bookkeepers or the *accountant mails* the statement.

Now consider this sentence:

Either of those desks *is* fine.

In this tricky example, *either* means "either one." The phrase "of those desks" describes, or modifies, *either,* which is the subject of the sentence.

PRACTICE 2

Choose the correct verb for each of the following sentences.

1. Each of the committee members (attend, attends) monthly meetings.
2. Everyone (bring, brings) (his/her, their) own unique talents to the project.
3. Anybody who (do, does) (his/her, their) best is appreciated.
4. None of us (has, have) experience with that computer program.
5. None of us (has, have) worked on a Macintosh computer before.
6. Somebody always (disagree, disagrees) with me.
7. Some people always (disagree, disagrees) with me.
8. A few people always (disagree, disagrees) with me.
9. Either Ahmed or Nick (is, are) getting the promotion.
10. Either of the applicants (is, are) a good choice.
11. Either the blanket or the booties (is, are) a cute gift for Shu's baby.
12. Either flowers or a box of candy (is, are) a perfect get well gift.

Special Case: Review of the Verb Forms of "to Be"

The verb *to be* often confuses people. The following chart shows the correct uses of the present tense forms of *to be.* Note that "you is" is never correct. Whether *you* refers to one person or twelve, *you are* is the correct form. Note, too, that *they are* is correct. *They is* is never acceptable.

Singular	Plural
I am	we are
you are	you are
he, she, it (name) is	they are

These are the past tense forms of the verb *to be*:

Singular	Plural
I was	we were
you were	you were
he, she, it (name) was	they were

Note that *was* is correct only when used with *I, he, she, it*, or *one person's name*. The same rule applies to the verb *to have*. Note when *has* is used.

Singular	Plural
I have	we have
you have	you have
he, she, it has	they have

Past tense is easier. Everyone *had*.

Singular	Plural
I had	we had
you had	you had
he, she, it had	they had

PRACTICE 3

Circle the correct verb in each sentence below.

1.   I (has, have) a good job.
2.   Hassan (has, have) his own restaurant.
3.   You (is, are) going to assist Luna in the upcoming project.
4.   She (is, are) the right person for the job.
5.   Darryl (is, are) running the new ad campaign.
6.   We (is, are) proud of the work we do.
7.   It (is, are) a difficult task.
8.   They (is, are) good friends.

Special Case: Passive Voice

Passive voice, the other sentence pattern discussed in Chapter 6, changes the rules of subject-verb agreement. As a reminder, look at both sentence types below:

Active Voice: The company *offers* a comprehensive medical plan.

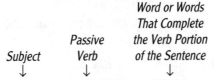

Passive Voice: A medical plan *is offered* by the company.

In the first sentence, the singular verb is *offers.* In the passive sentence, the rule for a singular verb changes. The passive verb is a combination of a form of *to be* (*am, is, are, was, were*) with a verb ending in *ed* or *en.*

A survey *was taken* of all employees.
A survey *was taken* of all employees by the public relations department.
The flight *was booked* last week.
The flight *was booked* last week by Mr. Rivera's secretary.

Compare the above passive sentences to their comparable active sentences. Note the changes in the verbs.

The public relations department *took* a survey of all employees.
Mr. Rivera's secretary *booked* the flight last week.

(Note: Using action verbs makes your writing stronger. Whenever you can, use verbs that describe action *instead of* using forms of the verb *to be* or *to have.* For example: Instead of writing

Julie *is* a good artist.

write

Julie *paints* beautiful pictures.)

PRACTICE 4

Step 1: Write "P" next to each passive-voice sentence and "A" next to each active-voice sentence.

Step 2: Make the passive sentences into active sentences. Remember: Passive-voice sentences may have the actor—but not up front. If there is no person or thing performing the action, you will have to make one up.

For example:

passive: The files were downloaded.

add person doing the action (still passive): The files were downloaded *by Ari*.

sentence changed to active voice: Ari downloaded the files.

1. The performance review is being given next week.
2. The supplies were purchased online.
3. The files were destroyed by a computer virus.
4. The sandwiches were brought in by Terrence.
5. Shu filed the motion in court.
6. The manager said to come in by 9:00.
7. Toni's party was given by Monica.

Special Case: Verb Agreement

When more than one verb is used in a sentence or paragraph, the time, or tense, must be consistent throughout. Read the following paragraph:

Yesterday, I interviewed several applicants for the administrative assistant position. The first woman walks into my office, sits down at the head of the conference table, and began interrogating me about our vacation policy. I sit there staring until she finishes, and then say, "Thank you for an informative discussion," stand up, and showed her to the door.

Yesterday sets the paragraph in the past. All verbs should remain in that tense. See the correct version below:

Yesterday, I interviewed several applicants for the administrative assistant position. The first woman *walked* into my office, *sat* down at the head of the conference table, and *began* interrogating me about our vacation policy. I *sat* there staring until she *finished,* and then *said,* "Thank you for an informative discussion," *stood* up, and *showed* her to the door.

Modifiers

A modifier is a word that gives more information about another word or phrase. The basic rule is to keep your modifier close to that word or phrase. Though there are many kinds of modifiers and complex rules, you can usually rely on common sense to keep your modifiers in the right place. A modifier belongs as close as possible to the word it is describing. In the example below, the modifier is misplaced:

> Throw me down the stairs my coat.

What happened? In this sentence, what should be thrown? My coat. Where should it be thrown? Down the stairs. To whom should it be thrown? Me. *My coat* is the descriptive phrase. It's what I want thrown, and should be placed close to the verb, *throw*.

> *Throw my coat* down the stairs to me.

What about this one?

> *Throw* momma from the train a *kiss.*

In this sentence, what should be thrown? A kiss.

> *Throw* a *kiss* to momma from the train.
> *Throw* momma a *kiss* from the train.

In the second example, *momma* is between *throw* and a *kiss*, but they are close enough to keep the meaning clear. (Momma doesn't get thrown from the train!)

PRACTICE 5

Rewrite the following paragraph, correcting misplaced modifiers. (Just use your common sense to find where some of these sentences went wrong.)

> Mr. Johnson placed in the hall the water cooler. It used to be in the reception area, but the cooler was a place to congregate and it got too crowded with so many salespeople in at once. The receptionist called this problem to Mr. Johnson's attention at a meeting of water cooler congregants.

Pronouns

Although many people are easily confused by pronouns, the rules for correct usage are easy to master. There are pronouns that *act,* those that *receive action*, and those that *own*.

Pronouns that act	Pronouns that receive action	Pronouns that own
I	me	my, mine
you	you	your, yours
he, she, it	him, her	his, her, hers, its
we	us	our, ours
they	them	their, theirs
who	whom	whose

Now, let's see them in context.

> Mary and I (not *me*) found last year's seminar more valuable than this year's.
> I gave John and him (not *he*) the first lunch.
> Whom (not *who*) can we blame?
> I am very concerned about the effect *your* (not *you*) smoking will have on my health.

Often, pronoun errors are made when the pronoun appears with a noun.

> Elsie and I share an apartment.

You would not say "me share," so you would not say "*Elsie and me* share." Remember the purpose of the pronoun in the sentence. If it is performing an action, it must come from the action column on the chart. Sometimes people think action pronouns sound more correct. Have you heard this one?

> John gave the keys to he and I.

The pronouns in this sentence are receiving the action and, therefore, should be *him and me*. *He* and *I* must *do* the giving.

More Pronoun Tips

Sometimes you have to complete a sentence in your head to choose the right pronoun.

> John is a better programmer than I (am).

Once you add the *am*, you won't make the mistake of saying:

> John is a better programmer than me (am).

When you talk about someone's smoking, jogging, typing, cooking, and so on, you are talking about a *thing*, not an action. So you wouldn't say,

> Mary hates him smoking.

You would say,

> Mary hates his smoking.

Just remember to use the pronoun that means ownership in these cases.

PRACTICE 6

Select the correct word to complete each sentence.

1. David and (*I, me*) are going to the outdoor concert.
2. Those reports are for Robert and (*I, me*).
3. (*We, Us*) and (*they, them*) are meeting at McDonald's at 6:00.
4. (*Who, Whom*) called while I was at the meeting?
5. Did you buy a wedding gift for José and (*she, her*)?
6. To (*who, whom*) should I send these invitations?
7. The company baseball team wants Sarah and (*I, me*) to join next season.
8. Gina understands the new office equipment better than (*I, me*).
9. Sandy and (*I, me*) share the locker.
10. I am very concerned about (*you, your*) not keeping a record of expenses.

More About Pronouns

Clarity in writing demands that pronoun references be clear. Your reader needs to know which noun the pronoun refers to. If that isn't immediately evident, the reader has to search back and forth over the sentence, trying to tie the pronoun to a preceding word. Searching delays comprehension.

Although Rizzo recently joined Winston on the project, *he* will still report to the president.

Who is *he*? Rizzo? Winston? Here's the correction:

Although Rizzo recently joined Winston on the project, *Winston* will still report to the president.

And another example:

Marlene told Judy she was tired and wouldn't go to the meeting.

Who is tired? Marlene? Judy? It is clearer as:

Because Marlene was tired, she told Judy she wouldn't go to the meeting.

Yet another example:

He dropped the calculator on the glass-topped desk and broke it.

What broke? The calculator? The desk? It is better as:

When he dropped the calculator on the glass-topped desk, the glass broke.

or

He dropped the calculator on the glass-topped desk, breaking the glass.

Avoid using a pronoun for which there is no clear reference. Beware of sentences that begin with *this,* because the tendency is to forget that *this* must relate to something specific.

No: We sold more machinery than anyone else in the field. *This* helped us gain national recognition.
Yes: We sold more machinery than anyone else in the field. *Our sales* helped us gain national recognition.

Avoid placing a pronoun too far from the word to which it refers. The meaning—the connection—will not be clear.

The graph at the end of the report was included in *its* original format.

To what does *its* refer? The report? The graph? Place *its* close to *graph,* the word to which *its* refers.

The graph, in its original format, was included at the end of the report.

PRACTICE 7

In the following sentences, correct the errors in pronoun usage.
1.   As each director arrives at the meeting, give them a financial statement.
2.   Jan wrote the agenda with Betty, but she was ill and couldn't attend the meeting.
3.   We wrote the sales presentation and produced the manual. It was a long one.
4.   Before word processors, managers had to wait for a secretary to type a memo, but now managers find that they shorten the time it takes to send a message from one office to another.
5.   Do not touch the magnetic surface of the diskette. This is so the oil from your fingertips won't get into the small holes in the plastic jacket.

Pronoun Agreement

Just as you checked at the beginning of the chapter for subject-verb agreement, it is important to make sure that pronouns agree with the subject. In the examples below, *his,* a singular pronoun, refers to *Max,* a singular subject. *Their* (a plural pronoun) refers to *employees* (a plural subject):

Max uses that program to edit *his* reports.
Our employees use that program to edit *their* reports.

When writing or speaking, people can easily change *person*, in other words, jump from second to third person pronouns:

> People should schedule important meetings early in the day because you are more alert during the early part of the work day.

The pronoun *you* refers to people. The correct pronoun is *they*. Look at the next example:

> One should button your jacket when giving a formal presentation.

Here is the correction:

> One should button *one's* (or *his/her*) jacket when giving a formal presentation.

If *you* start, *you* finish. Compare the following:

> Incorrect: You can't enter the Senate Chamber unless someone has a pass.
> Correct: You can't enter the Senate Chamber unless *you* have a pass.

PRACTICE 8

In the following sentences, correct the errors in pronoun agreement.

1. People should never play the stock market with more than you can afford to lose.
2. You can give your opinion to someone, but they don't have to accept it.
3. One should always think carefully before you criticize.
4. Emil sometimes rambles on long after the other person has turned their mind to other things.
5. If you are going to use inline skates, people should be careful and use your protective gear.
6. People should be careful what you wish for; they just might get it!

Run-on Sentences

A run-on sentence occurs when two complete thoughts are joined together, or run on, without correct punctuation.

> Most Scots are descended from their invaders these invaders included Celts, Norsemen, and Romans.

> Scotland has a population of more than 5 million people three fourths of the people live in the crowded Central Lowlands.

To correct a run-on sentence you have several choices:

1. You can decide to have two separate sentences.
   Most Scots are descended from their invaders. These invaders included Celts, Norsemen, and Romans.
2. If the thoughts are closely related, you can join the two with a semicolon.
   Most Scots are descended from their invaders; these invaders included Celts, Norsemen, and Romans.
3. You can join the sentences with a comma and a word that coordinates the two thoughts. Choose from these words: *and, but, or, for, not, yet, so.*
   Scotland has a population of over 5 million, but three fourths of the people live in the crowded Central Lowlands.
4. Finally, you can combine both thoughts, having only one subject and verb for the sentence.
   Most Scots are descended from their invaders, including the Celts, Norsemen, and Romans.

PRACTICE 9

Correct these run-on sentences.

1. You'll have to discuss your vacation time with the personnel department they make the vacation schedule.
2. I'm a student at Michigan State University my major is engineering.
3. When you make a recommendation, describe the present situation consider other courses of action.
4. Dr. Malcolm Brown has been named Chief of Surgery Dr. Susan Lovett has become Medical Director.
5. Communication between lawyer and client is privileged so is communication between doctor and patient.

Sentence Fragments

In most circumstances, you will use complete sentences. We say *most* because there are times when this isn't true. For example, in conversation, we frequently use sentence fragments or even just single words.

"Ready?"
"Now?"
"Yes?"

In fiction, a series of fragments creates a special effect.

There. I finally found grandfather. *Still wearing the same gray coat. The same shabby hat.*

You understand from the context that grandfather was still wearing the same gray coat, the same shabby hat. The italic portions, however, are not complete sentences. They cannot stand independently, as complete sentences can. Occasionally, even in memos, letters, and reports, the writer may use a single word or other fragment to emphasize a point or to change the pace.

Caution! Don't forget to attach your bills when you request repayment.

But when fragments appear again and again in business communications or school reports, they lose their punch. The reader can conclude only that the writer can't distinguish between a sentence fragment and a complete sentence.

What is a sentence fragment? A sentence fragment is a group of words that does not meet the minimum sentence requirements.

I saw him. *Standing at the water cooler.*

The first, three-word sentence satisfies minimum sentence requirements.

Subject	Active Verb	Object
↓	↓	↓
I	saw	him.

The sentence fragment that follows, however, does not have a subject, that is, does not tell *who* was standing at the water cooler. In fact, this fragment depends upon the sentence that comes before it for its meaning. This example gives us the second part of the definition of a sentence fragment: a group of words that depends upon an independent thought for completion. Let's look at that sentence, in corrected form.

I saw him standing at the water cooler.

By attaching *standing at the water cooler* to the independent thought, the writer has formed a complete sentence.

Sometimes a group of words looks like a complete sentence but, in fact, is a clause. A *clause* is a group of words that has a subject and a verb, but not all clauses are complete sentences.

Home heating costs have gone up. *Because the cost of oil has risen sharply.*

Notice that the group of words in italics has a subject (*cost*) and a verb (*has risen*). But this clause cannot stand alone; it depends upon the preceding thought for completion. Unless it is corrected, it remains a sentence fragment.

Be alert for words that introduce dependent clauses. (A dependent clause is one that cannot stand on its own.)

Examples of such words are:

after	if	when	whom	which
although	while	who	whose	that

Unless they are used properly, these words may signal that you've written a sentence fragment.

PRACTICE 10

Join the dependent clause to the independent clause, or rewrite the dependent clause to make it independent.

1. The project director walked out of the meeting. Which was his way of avoiding the disagreement.
2. I try to counsel him about his work problems. When he needs my help.
3. Meet us at the worksite. After you return from the bank.
4. Some of the orders are sent directly to our customers. While others are picked up at the plant.
5. We'll send the order directly to you. That being the case.

PRACTICE 11

Apply what you've learned in this chapter to correct the following sentences.

1. We've just hired Daniel Callaghan. Whom we've known for several years.
2. Tom Redding told us that you are buying XYZ Corporation, we wish you success with your new venture.
3. The operator connects the calls by pushing a button. Using the Light-Up switchboard.
4. The thalamus, fornix and mammillary body make memory possible. They are parts of the brain.
5. Either the underchefs or the head chef plan the meals.
6. Scientists now need to learn why the cells that control the disease dies.
7. Tallia is a more likely candidate than me.
8. The boss told me about you oversleeping.
9. All of my coworkers has the combination to the safe.
10. Either Jack or his roommates is responsible for the vandalism to the apartment.

ANSWERS

PRACTICE 1

The subway platform is very crowded at 8 A.M. Tourists *rush* to get started early. Many of the businesspeople *attempt* to get to their offices before 9 A.M., and workers returning from the 12 A.M. shift also *crowd* the platform. One of the conductors is especially interesting to watch during this hectic time. He *shouts* directions and *signals* with his hands as though he were a performer in a Broadway show. Crowds of people *stop* in their haste to observe this showman. One of the commuters *offers* coffee to him each morning. Without skipping a beat, he *accepts* it with a wink of thanks.

PRACTICE 2

1. Each of the committee members attends monthly meetings.
2. Everyone brings his/her own unique talents to the project.
3. Anybody who does his/her best is appreciated.
4. None of us has experience with that computer program.
5. None of us has worked on a Macintosh computer before.
6. Somebody always disagrees with me.
7. Some people always disagree with me.
8. A few people always disagree with me.
9. Either Ahmed or Nick is getting the promotion.
10. Either of the applicants is a good choice.
11. Either the blanket or the booties are a cute gift for Shu's baby.
12. Either flowers or a box of candy is a perfect get well gift.

PRACTICE 3

1. I have a good job.
2. Hassan has his own restaurant.
3. You are going to assist Luna in the upcoming project.
4. She is the right person for the job.
5. Darryl is running the new ad campaign.
6. We are proud of the work we do.
7. It is a difficult task.
8. They are good friends.

PRACTICE 4

1. *P* Active sentence: *Mrs. Brenner* is giving the performance review next week.
2. *P Mable* purchased the supplies online.
3. *P The computer virus* destroyed the files.
4. *P Terrence* brought in the sandwiches.
5. *A*
6. *A*
7. *P Monica* gave Toni's party.

PRACTICE 5

Answers will vary. Just be sure that your meaning is clear.

The water cooler used to be in the reception area, but because the salespeople congregate around it, the reception area got too crowded. At a meeting, the receptionist called the problem of the water cooler congregants to Mr. Johnson's attention. He moved the water cooler into the hall.

PRACTICE 6

1. David and *I* are going to the outdoor concert.
2. Those reports are for Robert and *me*.
3. *We* and *they* are meeting at McDonald's at 6:00.
4. *Who* called while I was at the meeting?
5. Did you buy a wedding gift for José and *her?*
6. To *whom* should I send these invitations?
7. The company baseball team wants Sarah and *me* to join next season.
8. Gina understands the new office equipment better than *I*.
9. Sandy and *I* share the locker.
10. I am very concerned about *your* not keeping a record of expenses.

PRACTICE 7

1. As each director arrives at the meeting, give him/her a financial statement.
2. Jan wrote the agenda with Betty, but Betty was ill and couldn't attend the meeting.
3. We wrote the sales presentation and produced the long manual.
4. Before word processors, managers had to wait for a secretary to type a memo, but now managers find that the word processors shorten the time it takes to send a message from one office to another.
5. Do not touch the magnetic surface of the diskette. Careful handling will prevent the oil from your fingertips from getting into the small holes in the plastic jacket.

PRACTICE 8

1. People should never play the stock market with more than they can afford to lose.
2. You can give your opinion to people, but they don't have to accept it.
   or You can give your opinion to someone, but he or she doesn't have to accept it.
3. One should always think carefully before one criticizes.
   or You should always think carefully before you criticize.
4. Emil sometimes rambles on long after the other person has turned his or her mind to other things.
   or Emil sometimes rambles on long after other people have turned their minds to other things.
5. If you are going to use inline skates, you should be careful and use your protective gear.
   or If people are going to use inline skates, they should be careful and use their protective gear.
6. People should be careful of what they wish for; they just might get it!
   or You should be careful of what you wish for; you just might get it!

PRACTICE 9

Answers will vary.

1. You'll have to discuss your vacation time with the Personnel Department; they make the vacation schedule.
2. I'm a student at Michigan State University, majoring in engineering.
3. When you make a recommendation, describe the present situation and consider other courses of action.
4. Dr. Malcolm Brown has been named Chief of Surgery; Dr. Susan Lovett has become Medical Director.

5. Just as communication between lawyer and client is privileged, so is communication between doctor and patient.

PRACTICE 10
Answers will vary.
1. To avoid the disagreement, the project director walked out of the meeting.
2. I try to counsel him about his work problems when he needs my help.
3. Meet us at the worksite after you return from the bank.
4. Some of the orders are sent directly to our customers, while others are picked up at the plant.
5. We'll send the order directly to you, that being the case.

PRACTICE 11
Answers will vary.
1. We've just hired Daniel Callaghan, whom we've known for several years.
2. Tom Redding told us that you are buying XYZ Corporation. We wish you success with your new venture.
3. Using the Light-Up switchboard, the operator connects the calls by pushing a button.
4. The thalamus, fornix, and mammillary body, all parts of the brain, make memory possible.
5. Either the underchefs or the head chef plans the meals.
6. Scientists now need to learn why the cells that control the disease die.
7. Tallia is a more likely candidate than I.
8. The boss told me about your oversleeping.
9. All of my coworkers have the combination to the safe.
10. Either Jack or his roommates are responsible for the vandalism to the apartment.

8.

Choose Your Words _____

Language Problems

You can expect the first draft of your letter, memo, or report to suffer from language problems: wordiness and repetition, trite or overused words, stilted phrases, clichés, and pretensions. Remember that, before you raced through your first draft, even before you jotted down all the thoughts in your brainstorming outline, you put the editor out of the room. You were in the process of creating, not correcting. Ultimately, though, writing is a process of simplification. The editor must return to simplify and clarify what the creator has written.

Wordiness

In Chapter 6, you practiced simplifying sentences. Such an important concept bears repeating because no reader wants to waste time extracting the meaning of sentences filled with unnecessary words. As you read the examples below, remember what a wise English teacher once said: "After you've finished editing your work, go back and take two or three *more* words out of every sentence."

Here are some examples of wordiness and repetition with their corrected forms:

No: Today in our modern world we can offer new products at competitive prices.
Yes: Today we can offer new products at competitive prices.

Note that "today" means the same as "modern world."

No: These are the basic essentials of our plan.
Yes: These are the essentials of our plan.

Note that, by definition, "essentials" are basic.

PRACTICE 1

In the following sentences, eliminate the words that aren't necessary to the meaning.

1. Even after the machine stopped, smoke was visible to the eye.
2. I have had no experience as yet.
3. If you don't understand an abbreviation, refer back to the index.
4. Rewrite the introduction again before you go on.

5. First and foremost, I want to commend your department.

6. Our study group reached a consensus of opinion.

7. Advanced planning was credited with saving the company.

8. Our product is totally unique.

9. The reason is because it would cost too much to replace the old equipment.

10. The battle produced gains that were small in size.

Stilted Phrases

Have you avoided words that some writers seem to save for letters, memos, and reports? Business letters are frequently filled with legal language as well as archaic words and phrases, even though they add no meaning. This example illustrates that point: "Enclosed herein please find my check... ." Ask yourself, "Would I use this terminology in conversation or on any other occasion?" If the answer is no, strike that cumbersome phrase from your work.

Here are some other examples of stilted, out-of-date, and overformal phrases that creep into business and report writing:

Don't Use	Substitute
Due to the fact	Because
Attached herewith	Here is
Am in receipt of	Have received
In reference to	Concerning
At the present time	Now
Under separate cover	Separately
Thanking you in advance	Thank you
At this point in time	Now
Be that as it may	But
By the same token	Also
Needless to say	(Nothing)

PRACTICE 2

Substitute plain English for the stilted language used in the following sentences.

1. In the process of checking your account, we have found that your bill is overdue.

2. Attached please find my check for $42.37.

3. I will take your plan under advisement.

4. We beg to advise you that our product will be on sale in May.

5. I am in receipt of your letter and its contents are noted.

6. We cannot decide whether or not we should enlarge the plant at this point in time.

7. Our inquiry is in reference to your first order only.

8. You can expect the catalogue to arrive under separate cover.

9. Some people came to the New World due to the fact that they wanted religious freedom.

10. It is often the case that business and labor leaders have much to learn about negotiating.

Redundancies

Do you use phrases that you've heard so many times you no longer think of the meaning? Are some of those phrases redundant if you stop to think about them?

Don't Use	Substitute
Consensus of opinion	Consensus, Agreement
Conclusive proof	Proof
Exactly identical	Identical
Positive identification	Identification
Reiterate again	Reiterate
Round in shape	Round

PRACTICE 3

Substitute a precise word or a simpler word for the underlined word or words in each sentence.

1. The bookcase is <u>green in color.</u>

2. Please <u>refer back</u> to the statements made on page 1.

3. It is my <u>personal opinion</u> that we need to have monthly meetings.

4. Robert and I have the <u>exact same</u> complaints about the new management.

5. The memo gave an <u>advance warning</u> that no one would be admitted to the meeting late.

Clichés and Pretensions

Did you use words that everyone has already used many times before? Are those words stilted and stuffy? These pretentious words remain in common use today, but you'll improve your writing if you don't overuse these terms, or better yet, if you choose simpler, more precise terms.

Don't Overuse	Substitute
Utilize	Use
Maximize	Increase
Finalize	Finish
Prioritize	Rank
Optimize	Cut the cost, improve
Profitwise	Profit

Due to

Due to is another overused, stilted phrase, and is also sometimes misused. There are many possible alternatives to *due to*. It is usually best to choose from one of the following:

being	because	as a result of	attributed to
in view of	caused by	given that	although
in line with	resulting from	despite	by

PRACTICE 4

To practice using alternatives, substitute a precise word or a simpler word for the underlined word or words in each sentence.

1. We need to systematize our files so that we can utilize them easily.
2. A larger sales force will maximize our benefits profitwise.
3. Your report legitimizes our belief that monthly meetings will optimize productivity.
4. When you prioritize and finalize your plans, let me know.

Words and Phrases to Avoid

Some incorrect words and phrases are used so frequently that we may begin to think they are *correct*. No matter how often we hear them, however, these expressions are not acceptable English. In *My Fair Lady*, Eliza Doolittle's dialect labeled her as "lower class"; similarly, the use of certain words and phrases can label us as "uneducated." This may sound unfair, but most employers are looking for people who can give their businesses a good image. *Ain't* won't do it.

1. ***ain't***

    We used to be able to say, "*Ain't* ain't in the dictionary." Now it is! Nevertheless, it is slang and should never be used in writing. *Ain't* is used incorrectly in place of *am not, is not, isn't, are not, aren't*.

2. *not no*

This is called a double negative and is used incorrectly in place of just *not* or *no*. Not only is this usage incorrect, but technically, two negatives make a statement *positive*!

Example: I'm *not no* mind reader.

Correct form: I'm *not* a mind reader or I'm *no* mind reader.

3. *could of*

This is incorrect usage. The correct term is *could have*.

Example: I *could have* danced all night.

4. *disregardless, irregardless*

These forms are incorrect. The word you want is *regardless*.

Example: Regardless of the weather, I plan to wear my new suit.

5. *graduate high school (or college)*

You did not *graduate* high school; you *graduated from* high school (or any other school).

6. *anywheres*

There is no such word as *anywheres*. Use *anywhere*.

Example: Marlene can't find her glasses *anywhere*.

7. *nowheres*

This is incorrect usage. Use *nowhere*.

Example: This debate is going *nowhere*.

8. *off of*

Omit the word *of*.

Example: He climbed *off* the bleachers.

PRACTICE 5

Rewrite each sentence correctly.

1. This project is going nowheres.

_____

2. He ain't a very good businessman.

_____

3. Wilma could of had the promotion if she had wanted it.

_____

4. Please take your feet off of my desk.

_____

5. I graduated high school in 1998.

_____

6. Irregardless of your opinion, I plan to hire the person I interviewed on Tuesday.

_____

Commonly Confused Words

Many English words that sound alike are different in both spelling and meaning. These easily confused words are called *homonyms*. For example:

> Lower back *pain* is a common ailment.
> The school board recommended that the children who had broken the windows pay for each *pane* that had to be replaced.

> The wooden *board* served as a temporary desk.
> I'm always *bored* at our long staff meetings.

Other frequently confused words sound almost alike. For example:

> Members of the council have agreed to *adopt* the proposal. (To *adopt* is to accept.)
> To succeed, you have to *adapt* to new conditions easily. (To *adapt* is to adjust to change.)
> The memo made an *allusion* to past product overruns. (An *allusion* is an indirect reference.)
> The company is under the *illusion* that increased sales will improve its profit statement. (An *illusion* is an incorrect belief or perception.)

Finally, there are words that don't sound at all alike but whose meanings are often confused. For example:

> If the bank decides to *lend* us money, we'll hire the personnel we need.
> You may want to *borrow* from our library.

We were *eager* to begin the trip we had planned for more than a year.
(*eager* = impatient, enthusiastic, hopeful)
The child's parents were *anxious* about the diagnosis.
(*anxious* = worried)

In the following list, you'll find examples of correct usage for many commonly confused words.

1. ***accept—except***
   I *accept* at least one delivery each day.
   Everyone *except* John left the meeting.

2. ***adapt—adopt***
   When visiting a foreign country, you must *adapt* to the local customs.
   Our company plans to *adopt* a new sales program.

3. ***advice—advise***
   Because of Marla's excellent *advice,* Coady completed a successful business deal.
   Marla *advised* Coady to be cautious.

4. ***affect—effect***
   The accident did not *affect* Darin.
   The *effect* on his brother, however, was great.
   Can the mediator *effect* a compromise on the wage issue?

5. ***aggravate—annoy***
   Government spending *aggravates* the enormous deficit.
   Having to leave my desk to find supplies *annoys* me.

6. ***all ready—already***
   Call me when the group is *all ready* to go.
   By the time the guest of honor arrived, we had *already* finished dinner.

7. **all right (Alright *is not an acceptable word.)***
   Is it *all right* to leave this window open?

8. ***all together—altogether***
   The four of us were *all together* at the coffee shop.
   This book is *altogether* too long.

9. ***allusion—illusion***
   I am amused at your *allusion* to my cooking as similar to fast food.
   You have the *illusion* that I enjoy that kind of music; I don't.

10. *altar—alter*

The wedding group stood in front of the *altar.*

Would it be inconvenient for you to *alter* your plans for this weekend?

11. *among—between*

The campaign director divided the state *among* the *three* most competent assistants.

The care of the children is often divided *between* the *two* parents.

12. *amount—number*

You would not believe the *amount* of time I have spent on this project!

I wish I could count the *number* of hours I have spent.

13. *angry at—angry with*

Ira was *angry at* the thought of working overtime.

Ira was *angry with* his boss for insisting that Ira work overtime.

14. *anxious—eager*

I am *anxious* about my child's illness.

I am *eager* to see your new car.

15. *as—like*

The radio station, *as* it did last year, sponsored the debate.

Paula looks very much *like* her sister.

16. *ascend—ascent—assent*

The aircraft *ascended* above the city.

The *ascent* to the tower was steep.

Because I value your opinion, I won't go ahead with the project without your *assent.*

17. *awful—very—real—really*

This fish tastes *awful.*

This fish tastes *very* bad.

Is this gold *real* or imitation?

Its shine is *really* bright.

18. *beside—besides*

Linda sat *beside* Ellen in the cafeteria.

Who, *besides* Pam, is signed up for the company's exercise program?

19. *born—borne*

Our youngest child was *born* last month.

Zac has *borne* (carried) the burden by himself long enough.

20. *borrow from* (Borrow off *is unacceptable.*)

Mickey *borrowed* the soldering iron *from* Marc.

21. *borrow—lend—loan*

May I *borrow* your pocket calculator?
I can *lend* you my mechanical pencil.
I need a $500 *loan*.

22. *brake—break*

I prefer a bicycle with a foot *brake*.
Because he did not *brake* in time, Dante crashed into the tree.
If you are not careful, you will *break* that dish.

23. *bring—take*

Bring home the groceries. (The past tense of *bring* is *brought*; *brung* is never acceptable.)
Take the coupons to the supermarket.

24. *can—may*

Some fortunate people *can* arrange their time to include work and pleasure.
(*can* = have the ability to)
You *may* park here only after 3 P.M.
(*may* = have permission to)

25. *capital—capitol—Capitol*

Ricardo has 90 percent of the necessary *capital* for his new business venture.
The chapter titles were set in *capital* letters.
Trenton is the *capital* of New Jersey.
New Jersey's *capitol* building is in Trenton.
Did you visit the *Capitol* when you were in Washington, D.C.?

26. *cite—sight—site*

An attorney often *cites* previous cases to support an argument.
One of the most beautiful *sights* in the country is the Grand Canyon.
The alternative school will be built on this *site*.

27. *coarse—course*

This *coarse* fabric makes my skin itch.
That is an acceptable *course* of action.

28. complement—compliment

Ariel's skills *complement* those of the rest of the department.

I'd like to *compliment* you for doing such a thorough job.

29. continually—continuously

Clem is *continually* (frequently) late.

The alarm sounded *continuously* (without interruption) for ten minutes.

30. council—counsel

Our neighbor has just been elected to the town *council.*

If you feel troubled, seek a friend's *counsel.*

On the advice of *counsel,* he refused to answer.

31. credible—creditable—credulous

Because the defendants had a good alibi, their story seemed *credible.*

As a result of many hours of hard work, Jane presented a *creditable* report.

You're too *credulous*—you shouldn't believe everything you hear!

32. currant—current

His unusual recipe called for *currant* jelly.

Because the *current* was swift, the canoe was difficult to maneuver.

33. desert—dessert

The *desert* is very hot and dry.

More and more soldiers have been *deserting* the army.

We had applesauce for *dessert.*

34. die—dye

Eventually, every living thing *dies.*

Blocking is a new way to *dye* fabric.

35. discover—invent

The builders *discovered* oil on our land.

Eli Whitney *invented* the cotton gin.

36. disinterested—uninterested

As a *disinterested* observer, this witness can be expected to give honest testimony.

Because I was *uninterested* in the lecture, I paid no attention.

37. draw—drawer

Rose *draws* very well.

She keeps her art supplies in the top *drawer* of her desk.

38. emigration—immigration
The Harlows *emigrated* from England.
After *immigrating* to the United States, the Harlows settled in Kansas.

39. famous—infamous—notorious
One of the twins is a *famous* pianist.
The other, unfortunately, is an *infamous* (or *notorious*) car thief.

40. farther—further
My car can run *farther* on this brand of gasoline.
I cannot continue this discussion any *further*.

41. fewer—less
Gerry invited *fewer* people to her holiday party this year.
Since she moved from a house to an apartment, she has *less* space.

42. formally—formerly
Please dress *formally* for the wedding.
I was *formerly* employed by a jewelry company, but I am now working in a bank.

43. good—well
Murray has just gotten a *good* job.
Maria performed the job *well*.
The apple tastes *good*.
Sarah doesn't feel *well*. (*Well*, normally used to describe an action, is used to describe health. *Well* is the opposite of *ill*.)

44. grate—great
The continuous harsh sound *grated* on my nerves.
A *grate* in the sidewalk covered the opening to the electrical wires.
Ernest Hemingway was considered a *great* writer in his own lifetime.

45. healthful—healthy
Orange juice is *healthful*.
If you eat properly and exercise sufficiently, you probably will be *healthy*.

46. imply—infer
Although he did not state it directly, the manager *implied* that we were losing business to the competition.
From the mayor's impatient questions, we *inferred* that she wanted the project completed as quickly as possible.

47. *in—into*
Heather stood *in* the living room.
Pedro came rushing *into* the room.

48. *it's—its*
I think *it's* a fine idea!
The dog wagged *its* tail.

49. *kind of—sort of—type of*
(These expressions can be used interchangeably. They should never be followed by *a*.)
Mrs. Petrella always buys that *kind of* meat.
I like that *sort of* book.
This is my favorite *type of* record.

50. *later—latter*
Sue can finish the report *later* this week.
I can meet you Tuesday or Thursday, but the *latter* would be more convenient.

51. *lead—led*
I'll need one more *lead* pipe to complete this plumbing job.
I only enjoy a race when I am in the *lead.*
Lead the horse to water.
Hector was unfamiliar with that route, so Jules *led* the way.

52. *learn—teach*
I am having difficulty *learning* how to use the word processor.
Leslie is patiently trying to *teach* me how to use it.

53. *let—leave*
After the customs officer clears a traveler's baggage, the officer *lets* the traveler *leave* the area.

54. *loose—lose—loss*
Parents are usually excited about a child's first *loose* tooth.
If you step out of line, you will *lose* your place.
The company has recovered from last year's *loss* of profits.

55. *manor—manner*
The *manor,* or landed estate, dates back to feudal times in England.
A pleasant *manner* is especially helpful for a salesperson.

56. *miner—minor*

The coal *miners* struck for better medical care.
Many laws classify young people under eighteen as *minors*.
This *minor* problem will not cause delay.

57. *moral—morale*

Because of Ed's high *moral* standards, he returned the wallet to its owner.
The story of the boy who cried wolf has a *moral* that applies to everyone.
Because the war was *immoral*, the *morale* of the troops was low.

58. *nauseated—nauseous*

The odor of the skunk *nauseated* Sara.
When we drove past the skunk, the car was filled with a *nauseous* odor.

59. *pail—pale*

The paint is in one-gallon *pails*.
Maria's long illness left her complexion *pale*.

60. *passed—past*

We *passed* the Model T on the parkway.
Our profits increased by 17 percent during the *past* six months.

61. *peace—piece*

If we work together, perhaps we can achieve a lasting *peace*.
I jotted down some notes on a *piece* of paper.

62. *persecute—prosecute*

Older children frequently *persecute* their younger brothers and sisters.
If they violate the new law, they will be *prosecuted*.

63. *personal—personnel*

The items written in a diary are often highly *personal*.
When applying for a job at a large company, you must go to the *personnel* office.

64. *plain—plane*

The meaning is quite *plain* and requires no further explanation.
We rode for miles across the open *plains* of Kansas.
The *plane* landed smoothly.
Please *plane* that wood so that I can build a birdhouse with it.

65. practicable—practical

Studying computer programming is a *practicable* plan for the future.
(*practicable* = workable, feasible)
The decision to computerize the payroll was a *practical* one that should help lower our costs.
(*practical* = sensible)

66. precede—proceed

A preface *precedes* the first chapter of a book.
Don't let me interrupt you; *proceed* with your work.

67. principal—principle

A school is as good as its teachers and *principal.*
She is able to live on the interest from her savings and to leave the *principal* intact.
The *principal* actors in the play remained for a rehearsal of the second act.
The lever is the *principle* upon which many simple machines are based.

68. quiet—quite

Find a *quiet* place where you can study.
That is *quite* a strong accusation.

69. raise—rise

When we *raise* the flag, we'd like everyone in the audience to *rise.*

70. sit—set

The committee members were asked to *sit* down.
Please *set* those papers on my desk.

71. stationary—stationery

The price has remained *stationary;* it hasn't gone up or down.
We need a new logo for our business *stationery.*

72. sure—surely

I am *sure* that Alice will be at the meeting.
You *surely* don't expect me to take notes.

73. than—then

New York is smaller *than* Wyoming, but Wyoming is much less densely populated *than* New York.
First the eastern seaboard was colonized; *then* settlers moved westward.

74. *their—there—they're*

Employees can bring *their* children to the company's child-care center.
There must be an easier way to operate this machine.
As for the members of Congress, *they're* not always responsible for the wisest decisions.

75. *through—threw*

The crew worked *through* the night to repair the wires.
When the Little League pitcher *threw* the ball, her teammates cheered.

76. *to—too—two*

United States presidents often travel *to* foreign countries.
Many foreign heads of state visit the United States, *too.*
Two notable visitors were Thabo Mbeki and Tony Blair.

77. *vain—vane—vein*

You're not usually *vain;* why do you keep looking at yourself in the mirror?
A rooster is the traditional weather *vane* symbol.
Veins carry deoxygenated blood to the heart.

78. *wade—weighed*

The children *waded* near the shore.
The clerk *weighed* the fresh vegetables.

79. *waist—waste*

It makes sense to measure your *waist* before you buy a pattern.
We talked about the dangers of chemical *waste* sites.

80. *weather—whether*

What is the *weather* forecast for tomorrow?
Whether or not you wish to pay taxes, you must.

81. *who's—whose*

The sergeant asked, "*Who's* responsible for clean-up today?"
Do you know *whose* turn it is?

82. *writes—rights—rites*

Kurt Vonnegut *writes* excellent fiction.
Their attorney explained the family's *rights* in the lawsuit.
The religious *rites* of many Indian tribes are an impressive part of their culture.

83. *your—you're*

Where is *your* car parked?
You're doing a good job on the project.

PRACTICE 6

Circle the number of the incorrect word in each paragraph, and supply the right word. If there is no error, circle number 5.

1. Because I was <u>anxious</u> to avoid another argument, I <u>accepted</u> Roy's
          (1)   (2)

    apology. Since his story seemed <u>credible</u>, there was no point in carrying
                                                                (3)

    the argument any <u>further</u>.
                                  (4)

    <u>No error</u>
        (5)

2. Olivia left the elevator and <u>proceeded</u> to the <u>personal</u> office. The unfriendly
                                                      (1)   (2)

    interviewer lowered Olivia's <u>morale</u>, but she was still <u>eager</u> to obtain the job.
                                                  (3)   (4)

    <u>No error</u>
        (5)

3. The <u>effect</u> of the unusual visitor on the family was startling. Mother <u>adopted</u>
          (1)   (2)

    Mrs. Chuggley's speech habits; father <u>altered</u> his smoking habits to suit Mrs.
                                                        (3)

    Chuggley's allergy; and I found myself <u>continuously</u> saying, "Yes, ma'am."
                                                            (4)

    <u>No error</u>
        (5)

4. The <u>course</u> of action determined by the city <u>counsel</u> at its last meeting
          (1)   (2)

    has <u>already</u> begun to <u>affect</u> us. <u>No error</u>
          (3)   (4)   (5)

5. Family gatherings are always interesting. Grandpa is usually <u>angry with</u> Aunt
                                                                      (1)
   Celia. Inez insists upon <u>sitting</u> <u>besides</u> Grandma. Mother tries to divide her
                             (2)   (3)
   attention equally <u>among</u> all of the guests. <u>No error</u>
                       (4)   (5)

6. I was <u>altogether</u> shocked when Armando returned the ice bucket he had
           (1)
   <u>borrowed from</u> us last spring. When I <u>complemented</u> him for returning it
       (2)   (3)
   so promptly, Armando's red face told me that he understood my <u>implied</u>
                                                                    (4)
   sarcasm. <u>No error</u>
              (5)

7. Please put the change <u>into</u> your pocket before you <u>lose</u> it. It's hard enough to
                          (1)   (2)
   keep pace with today's prices without carelessly losing money. That <u>kind of</u>
                                                                          (3)
   negligence makes me <u>loose</u> my temper. <u>No error</u>
                         (4)   (5)

8. The <u>minor</u> <u>led</u> the team into the shaft. After several hours of dangerous work,
        (1)   (2)
   they <u>ascended</u> jubilantly. It had been a <u>really</u> terrifying experience. <u>No error</u>
          (3)   (4)   (5)

9. I am <u>formally</u> engaged in a program of good nutrition. I always eat a <u>healthy</u>
          (1)   (2)
   breakfast. I consume <u>fewer</u> sweets and I spend <u>less</u> time stalking the
                          (3)   (4)
   refrigerator for snacks. <u>No error</u>
                             (5)

10. Lea and her sister asked if they might go swimming at the pool. Although
    both of them <u>can</u> swim <u>quite</u> well, <u>their</u> mother refused permission. Sue was
                  (1)   (2)   (3)
    very angry and said they were being <u>prosecuted</u>. <u>No error</u>
                                          (4)   (5)

PRACTICE 7

In each group, circle the number of the sentence that contains an incorrectly used word and supply the correct word. If there is no error, circle number 5.

1. (1) The damage has all ready been done.

    (2) Mr. Kelley was altogether too surprised to speak.

    (3) Events have borne out my prediction.

    (4) Perry is an altar boy at Queen of Peace Church.

    (5) No error

2. (1) Please cite at least three examples.

    (2) The dealer was cited for contempt.

    (3) For that sight, we're planning a municipal parking lot.

    (4) When the bridge is within sight, look for our street.

    (5) No error

3. (1) Was his work all right?

    (2) They ordered six yards of plain fabric and ten yards of plaid.

    (3) Do they have the capitol to invest?

    (4) Our club has fewer members this year than last year.

    (5) No error

4. (1) I applied the brakes immediately.

    (2) Cars are borne across the river on a ferry.

    (3) Are you feeling all right?

    (4) When you are all ready, I will pick you up.

    (5) No error

5. (1) Do the typing first; finish the filing latter.

    (2) The envoy was received formally at the ambassador's home.

    (3) Our department had a loss, but the rest of the firm did well.

    (4) We could hear a vigorous discussion of current problems.

    (5) No error

6. (1) When you give your report, be sure to cite as many concrete examples as possible.

    (2) "I am surely not guilty of excessive spending!" he shouted.

    (3) The new copier was delivered through the basement.

    (4) Because of several miner disagreements, the discussion came to a halt.

    (5) No error

7. (1) The consultant was asked to advise the planning board.

    (2) My advice is that construction of the bridge should be postponed.

    (3) She was hired because her experience would complement that of the rest of the staff.

    (4) Prospective homeowners are eager for reduction of the mortgage interest rate.

    (5) No error

8. (1) The attorney has placed the file for the Jones case in the bottom draw.

    (2) The senior citizen center will be formally opened next week.

    (3) Don't lose this pen; it is hard to replace.

    (4) Kareem is quite an athlete.

    (5) No error

9. (1) We have passed the goal we set for the second quarter.

    (2) There was nothing to do but accept the plan.

    (3) There is to much at stake to back down now.

    (4) The crowd was quiet until the rocket ascended.

    (5) No error

10. (1) The manager was pleased that you had done such a creditable job.

    (2) No one knew him as I did.

    (3) Choose your coarse of action and stick to it.

    (4) I think the skirt is too loose on you.

    (5) No error

PRACTICE 8

Circle the error in each incorrect sentence. If there is no error, put a "C" next to the sentence. Write the correct word to replace each error.

1. Ching wants to lend your calculator for a few days.   _____

2. Please contact me by phone.   _____

3. The book alluded in great depth to the Civil War.   _____

4. Company B's continued dumping of waste has aggravated the pollution problem.   _____

5. His foot tapping really aggravates me.   _____

6. Please rise your hand if you know the answer.   _____

7. She gives the allusion of being much thinner than she is.   _____

8. Bill sure doesn't want to work overtime.   _____

9. Lee promised to learn Eda English.   _____

10. George felt awful bad about the accident.   _____

Adapting to the Times

In the past, the following sentence would have been considered correct:

> Each member of the management team took *his* place at the conference table.

Today, that sentence would offend many readers because the writer uses the pronoun *his* to refer to both men and women. You see only a slight improvement in the alternative below:

> Each member of the management team took *his/her* place at the conference table.

On the one hand, the sentence grants existence to women on the management team; on the other hand, the sentence is awkward. Try this, instead:

> *Members* of the management team took *their* places at the conference table.

As you can see, the solution is using a plural subject (*Members*) rather than a singular subject (*Each member*). The plural pronoun *their* replaces *his*. Other simple changes will also help you keep sexism out of your writing. Follow these rules:

1. Do not add *-ess* to words that do not require that suffix. For example, *actor* means male actor and *actress* means female. *Manager,* however, means male or female manager.

2. When the word can be comfortably modified to be unisex, modify it. *Chairperson* sounds as legitimate as *chairman*. Other examples follow:

businessman	businessperson
cameraman	camera operator
fireman	firefighter
mailman	mail carrier
man	person, human being
man-hour	work-hour
manmade	artificial, synthetic
policeman	police officer
repairman	service representative
salesman	salesperson
	sales agent
	sales associate
workman	worker

ANSWERS

PRACTICE 1
1. Even after the machine stopped, smoke was visible.
2. I have had no experience.
3. If you don't understand an abbreviation, refer to the index.
4. Rewrite the introduction before you go on.
5. First, I commend your department.
6. Our study group reached a consensus.
7. Planning was credited with saving the company.
8. Our product is unique.
9. It would cost too much to replace the old equipment.
10. The battle produced small gains.

PRACTICE 2
1. Checking your account, we have found that your bill is overdue.
2. Here is my check for $42.37.
3. I will consider your plan.
4. Our product will be on sale in May.
5. I've received your letter.
6. We cannot decide whether we should enlarge the plant now.
7. Our inquiry concerns your first order only.
8. You can expect the catalogue to arrive separately.
9. Some people came to the New World because they wanted religious freedom.
10. Frequently, businesspeople and labor leaders have much to learn about negotiating.

PRACTICE 3
1. The bookcase is <u>green</u>.
2. Please <u>refer</u> to the statements made on page 1.
3. It Is my <u>opinion</u> that we need to have monthly meetings.
4. Robert and I have the <u>same</u> complaints about the new management.
5. The memo gave a <u>warning</u> that no one would be admitted to the meeting late.
   or The memo warned that no one would be admitted to the meeting late.

PRACTICE 4
1. We need to <u>organize</u> our files so that we can use them easily.
2. A larger sales force will <u>increase</u> our profits.
3. Your report <u>confirms</u> (<u>shows</u>) our belief that monthly meetings will <u>increase</u> productivity.
4. When you set your priorities and <u>finish</u> your plans, let me know.

PRACTICE 5
1. This project is going *nowhere.*
2. He *isn't* a very good businessman.
3. Wilma *could have* had the promotion if she had wanted it.
4. Please take your feet *off* my desk.

5.   I *graduated from* high school in 1998.
6.   *Regardless* of your opinion, I plan to hire the person I interviewed on Tuesday.

PRACTICE 6
1.   (1) eager
2.   (2) personnel
3.   (4) continually
4.   (2) council
5.   (3) beside
6.   (3) complimented
7.   (4) lose
8.   (1) miner
9.   (2) healthful
10.   (4) persecuted

PRACTICE 7
1.   (1) already
2.   (3) site
3.   (3) capital
4.   (5) No error
5.   (1) later
6.   (4) minor
7.   (5) No error
8.   (1) drawer
9.   (3) too
10.   (3) course

PRACTICE 8
1.   Ching wants to *borrow* your calculator for a few days.
2.   Please *communicate with* me by phone.
3.   The book *referred* to the Civil War in great depth.
4.   C
5.   His foot tapping really *annoys* me.
6.   Please *raise* your hand if you know the answer.
7.   She gives the *illusion* of being much thinner than she is.
8.   Bill *surely* doesn't want to work overtime.
9.   Lee promised to *teach* Eda English.
10.   George felt *very* (or *really*) bad about the accident.

PRACTICE 9
1.   Businesspeople and educators met to discuss the work-study program.
2.   All participants should meet the bus at their hotels.
3.   All the reporters returned to their newspaper offices.
4.   We expect a salesperson to call on our office monthly.
5.   At full capacity, our company employs four service representatives.

PRACTICE 10
I cannot emphasize enough that developing a business plan is not simply a technique to keep our finance department informed. To sell this company, we're going to have to show prospective buyers the direction the company will take in the next five years. For example, our buyer has the right to know about our new product plans as well as our strategies to increase our profit.

9.

Be a Good Mechanic

In this chapter we review the basic rules of punctuation, capitalization, and spelling and provide a brief overview of the major problems most writers have.

Punctuation

You probably know that a sentence begins with a capital letter and ends with a period, an exclamation point, or a question mark. But most of us encounter problems between that initial capital letter and the end mark. What words should be capitalized? When do you use a comma, a semicolon, a colon? Learning a few basic rules will help you answer these questions—and improve your writing skills.

The Comma

1. A comma separates two complete thoughts joined by a conjunction such as *and, but, or, not,* or *for.*

    We *moved* our offices to the sixteenth floor, and *we* now *enjoy* a wonderful view of the city.

    If each part of the sentence did not have a subject and a verb, the comma would be left out.

    We *moved* our offices to the sixteenth floor and now *enjoy* a wonderful view of the city.

2. An introductory word or group of words is usually followed by a comma.

    Generally, it is easier to get a job if you've had work experience.

    To complete the project, we had to work on the weekend.

    Since you will be working until 10 P.M., you may come in at 11 A.M. tomorrow.

    If the sentence is turned around, the comma is left out.

    You may come in at 11 A.M. tomorrow since you will be working until 10 P.M.

3. Commas set off words or groups of words that interrupt the flow of the sentence.

    The board of directors, *however,* will not approve the merger.

    Edmond Simpson, *the president of the local board of education,* has done a great deal for our schools.

    Before I continue, *dear friends,* let me thank you for coming here today.

    Note that two commas are required to set off an expression unless it comes at the beginning or the end of the sentence.

4. Commas separate three or more items in a series. A comma should come before the *and* between the last two items.

    Please order four dozen manila envelopes, a carton of letter-size file folders, *and* a thousand ballpoint pens.

    Although the comma before the last item is omitted sometimes, it is usually clearer to include it. Read the sentence below.

    We sent memos to personnel, engineering and maintenance managers.

    Are engineering and maintenance managers two different people? You can't tell from the way the sentence is punctuated.
    Insert a comma before *and* to show that three managers received memos.

    We sent memos to personnel, engineering, and maintenance managers.

5. A comma separates the day from the year and the year from the rest of the sentence.

    Lena began working on May 15, 1998, at the Positive Insurance Company's main office.

    The date on a letter or memo has this form:

    June 20, 2000

6. A comma separates the name of a city from the name of the state and the name of the state from the rest of the sentence.

    My next business trip is to *Detroit, Michigan,* and *Orlando, Florida.*

In the inside address of a letter, the city and state are separated by a comma. No punctuation comes between the state and the zip code.

Groton, Massachusetts 01450

San Diego, CA 92101

7.   A comma is used after the greeting in a friendly letter.

Dear Walter,

8.   A comma follows the closing in a friendly letter or a business letter.

Very truly yours,
William Baez

9.   A comma separates a direct quotation from the rest of the sentence.

"I put the file on the desk," the assistant said. The manager answered, "I'll look at it in a moment."

The Semicolon

1.   The semicolon connects two complete thoughts that are closely related.

The dinner was excellent; the service was awful.

2.   Sometimes a word such as *however, nevertheless,* or *therefore* follows the semicolon.

Ms. Steinberg liked your proposal; *however,* she cannot commit any more money at this time.

3.   The semicolon is used for clarity to separate complete thoughts that contain commas.

Since he arrived, my uncle has broken our coffee pot, the sofa bed, and the washing machine; but we really enjoy his company.

Quotation Marks

1.   Quotation marks separate the exact words of the speaker from the person who spoke them.

The manager said, "Is your plan feasible considering our resources?"

Note that the question mark is placed inside the quotation marks because it is part of the question being quoted.

2. Quotation marks also set off both parts of a broken quotation. Don't capitalize the first word of the second part of the quotation unless it is the beginning of a new sentence.

    "Once we've looked at your application," the admissions officer said, "we'll either accept you immediately or send you a deferral statement."

    "We've looked at your application," the admissions officer said. "We'll either accept you immediately or send you a deferral statement."

In both examples note that the comma and the period are inside the quotation marks.

The Colon

1. The colon is used to introduce a list (when the list is not preceded by a verb) or a formal quotation or statement.

    Please review the following factors: costs for the month, expenses for the month, and nonmonetary benefits for the month.

    The committee has reached an unfortunate conclusion: There is no easy way to save this company from bankruptcy.

    Exception: when the list is preceded by the verb *to be*

    The factors to review *are* costs for the month, expenses for the month, and nonmonetary benefits for the month.

    The unfortunate conclusion reached by the committee is that there *is* no easy way to save this company from bankruptcy.

2. The colon is used after the greeting in a business letter.

    Dear Ms. Patel:

The Hyphen

1. The hyphen is used to divide a word at the end of a line. Always divide a word between syllables. Use your dictionary to help you.

    All of the women in our department
    stay for the Tai Chi class on Thurs-
    day afternoons.

    Note: The last word of the first line (department) should *never* be hyphenated.

2. The hyphen divides compound numbers from *twenty-one* to *ninety-nine.*

    thirty-six, seventy-eight

3. The hyphen links two or more words to form a compound adjective.

    well-respected teacher

    free-floating currencies

    But note than an *–ly* compound adjective is *not* hyphenated.

    dearly loved child

    highly dangerous move

4. A compound adjective or noun formed by adding *self-* to another word is always hyphenated.

    self-reliant

    self-respect

5. The hyphen is used when adding some prefixes.

    ex-wife   non-European

The Apostrophe

1. An apostrophe shows that one or more letters have been omitted in a contraction.

    Janet *isn't* (is not) studying tonight.

    We'll (we will) call you at six o'clock.

2. An apostrophe shows possession. The apostrophe comes *before* the *s* in singular words and *after* the *s* in plural words. Exceptions are words made plural without an *s*.

    the baby's rattle (singular)

    the babies' rattles (plural)

    the administrator's meeting (singular)

    the administrators' meeting (plural)

    the woman's shoe (singular)

    the women's shoes (plural)

    the child's food (singular)

the children's food (plural)

Note that proper nouns, such as names, also follow the rule given above.

Mr. Jones's jacket   the Joneses' property

Mr. Martin's jacket   the Martins' property

Remember that a possessive pronoun never has an apostrophe.

hers   its   theirs   whose

3.   An apostrophe shows the plural of letters and numbers.

All *4's* are on the far court.

I never get *E's* when I play Scrabble.

Dashes

1.   Dashes emphasize an interruption within a sentence.

We planned the reception—a beautiful one—right after the ceremony.

2.   A dash is used before a word that sums up preceding items.

Warmth, flexibility, and compassion—these are the qualities this job requires.

Parentheses

Parentheses set off words not directly related to the main thought of the sentence. The information in parentheses is sometimes thought of as an "aside."

The lock on the front door (it was broken by a burglar) must be fixed.

The correspondence has been entered in the files (look under drawers A–K).

PRACTICE 1

Correctly punctuate each of the following sentences. Some sentences have more than one error. Some have no errors. If a sentence is correct, write C.

1.   Before leaving the office Mr. Tevis reviewed all of the days cases.

2.   He and I work for the same company and we take the train together.

3.   The chief administrator had wanted to interview Joan but was unable to keep the appointment.

4.   It isn't that we dont want to join you we just cant.

5. "If I had known you were serving dinner" said Isabel, I would not have eaten earlier.

6. Martin Haber my exboss was at the dinner.

7. When you arrive at the airport in Seattle Washington please give me a call.

8. Gregory Tesides the Symphony Club president and his wife a librarian chaired the benefit for the local hospital.

PRACTICE 2

Correctly punctuate each of the following sentences. Some sentences have more than one error. Look carefully for all possible items of punctuation.

1. The word processor can identify all the number 6s in the report.

2. While many people were concerned about minor pollutants such as solid waste the more serious problem of toxic waste surfaced.

3. College costs have risen to an all-time high said Chancellor Mendoza.

4. Motivation is not enough you must earn better grades.

5. Although Clara had expected some problems her new job as the deans assistant is challenging and rewarding.

6. That woman the one in the yellow dress is Sarahs mother.

7. Jake isnt working tonight but Keith will substitute for him.

8. Did you read the article about self styled nutrition experts?

9. When you are in Lincoln Nebraska you can visit a friend of mine.

10. Chuck Hardwick our local assemblyman is a very responsive and responsible legislator.

11. Some legislators however respond to mail only with form letters.

12. The shipment did arrive on time however several items we had ordered were not included.

13. I wont ask you again forget it.

14. If you thought thirty nine was a difficult birthday wait until you are forty nine.

15. Our department cant run effectively without the following supplies file folders address labels envelopes pencils a pencil sharpener and felt tip pens.

PRACTICE 3

Supply the missing punctuation in the following business letter.

July 12 2000

Ms. Hilda Blume
Wilson Supply Company
419 West Broad Street
Westfield New Jersey 07090

Dear Ms. Blume:
Since you and I spoke on June 24 I have decided to give our office supply order to your company. I assume that the terms we discussed during that conversation still apply.

Instead of waiting for your official order form I will place our order now. Please send us the following items
    3 reams of 20 lb. Paper
    6 dozen pencils number 2s
    1 box of Smiths Erasable Bond

Thank you for your immediate attention to this order.

I look forward to our working together. By the way the next time you are in our part of town with samples please call me.

Sincerely
Mary Ellen Collins

A Few Rules of Capitalization

The following items should be capitalized:

1. The first letter of the first word in a sentence

    Please complete the application today.

2. The first word of a direct quotation

    Ms. Selletti replied, "**W**e finished the report."

3. The word I

    Yesterday **I** spoke to the manager.

4. Names of persons, places, streets, organizations, languages, specific school courses, important historical events, and documents

    My friend **J**uanita **L**ee lives on **K**ingston **S**treet, in **C**leveland, **I**llinois. She is president of the **A**merican **C**ancer **S**ociety in her community, speaks **S**panish fluently, and teaches **M**odern **H**istory II at **W**ilson **H**igh **S**chool.

    The **E**mancipation **P**roclamation was signed during the **C**ivil **W**ar.

    Thomas **T**sing, manager of the **P**ersonnel **D**epartment at the **S**avalot **C**orporation, has been appointed to the company's **H**ealth and **S**afety **C**ommittee.

5. A brand name, but *not* the word that identifies the product

    I went to the drugstore to buy some **S**moothmore toothpaste and **F**lexo shampoo.

6. Days of the week, months, holidays

    Next **M**onday, **M**ay 30, will be **M**emorial **D**ay.

    The names of the seasons are *not* capitalized.

    I will graduate next *summer.*

7. *East, west, north,* and *south* when they designate sections of the country or are part of a place name, but *not* when they simply indicate direction

    I love the **W**est. When traveling *west* on Route 80, watch for the radar traps.
    She lives on **S**outh **B**ellview **D**rive.

8. The first word and each important word in a title of a book, play, magazine, poem, or other work

    Ernest Hemingway's novel ***A F**arewell to **A**rms* will always be my favorite.

9. The initials of a person's name

    J.C. Walinski

    Kim **K.** Sukihani

10. A personal title *only* when it comes before the name

    Robert Kerry became *captain* after **C**aptain Healey retired.

    Last week **M**rs. Laurel Golden was named *president* of the Red Cross. She was congratulated by **D**r. Carlos Reyes, the *secretary-treasurer* of the organization.

Note the following correct forms:

the secretary of state   the senator from Montana   the mayor of Atlanta

11.   The first word in each line of poetry

He walked amongst the trial men

In a suit of shabby gray.... .

12.   The names of the Deity

God   **A**llah

PRACTICE 4

To correct these sentences, either add or delete capital letters.

1.   Our company, Ralme, inc., moved its headquarters to Carson city, Nevada, in the Spring of 1982.

2.   We've asked Mr. Arthur Ralme to chair the Board of directors of Hewes Corporation.

3.   After we leave San Francisco, we'll travel in the orient for two weeks.

4.   Submit your bid to the department of transportation, Washington, D.C.

5.   First walk east on Main Street until you reach east fourth Avenue.

6.   Have you read the new book on management, *Making time make you money?*

PRACTICE 5

In the following instructions for taking telephone orders, supply the missing capital letters and remove the unnecessary ones.

1.   answer each call as quickly as possible.

2.   Determine that the caller is a Member.

a. Ask the caller for his/her name and address.

b. Insert facts into the Computer.

c. Ask the caller for his/her Membership Number and expiration Date.

d. Check these details with the Computer printout.

3.   Take the order. Enter the Order into the computer.

4.   Repeat the Order to the Customer.

These instructions take effect on february 1.

PRACTICE 6

Correct any capitalization errors in the following letter.

January 10, 2001

Mr. Lorenzo Mendoza
67 Main street
Wilmington, Delaware 19823

Dear Mr. Mendoza:

We are happy to confirm your family's Reservations for February 22–26, and are delighted to welcome you again this year. You requested two rooms on the Second Floor, which we will reserve for you.

Since last year, we've added many Winter Sports Activities. I'm sending you our new brochure, which describes these activities. I know that your family, in particular, will enjoy the night skiing.

If I can do anything else to help you plan your Vacation, please let me know.

sincerely,
Marge Browning

Spelling

For some people, correct spelling seems to come easily. For many others, spelling correctly takes persistent study. If you have trouble with spelling, try this approach to improve:

1. Use a small notebook to record the words you frequently misspell.
2. When you discover a problem word, write it in your notebook. Check a dictionary for the correct spelling, syllable division, and pronunciation.
3. Look at the word. Say it in syllables.
4. Try to apply one of the rules that follow to understand why the word is spelled as it is.
5. Close your eyes and picture the word.
6. Write the word. Check it. Rewrite it.
7. Review words you have already studied.

Learning to spell a long word is much easier if you divide it into syllables. For example:

con • tin • u • a • tion

Learn to spell each syllable and, finally, put the word together.

Adding Prefixes and Suffixes

Spelling problems sometimes occur when prefixes and suffixes are added to words. A *prefix* is a group of letters added to the *beginning* of a word to change its meaning. A *suffix* is a group of letters added to the *end* of a word to change its meaning. Sometimes the word to which a prefix or suffix is added is called the *root* word. For example:

Prefix	Root	Suffix
*dis*quiet	quiet	quiet*ly*

Most often, prefixes can be added to a word without changing the spelling of the root word. For example:

Prefix	(Meaning)	Word	Combination
un +	(not)	necessary =	unnecessary
ir +	(not)	reversible =	irreversible

A suffix that begins with a consonant doesn't change the spelling of most words. (A *consonant* is any letter that is not a vowel. The vowels are *a, e, i, o,* and *u.*) For example:

mortal	+	ly	= mortally
like	+	ness	= likeness

But there are some exceptions:

true	+	ly	= truly
due	+	ly	= duly

When you add a suffix beginning with a vowel to a word that ends in a consonant, the spelling of the root word usually doesn't change. For example:

port	+	able	= portable
economic	+	al	= economical

Suffixes *do* change the spelling of words that end in *y*: the y changes to *i*. For example:

defy +	ance	= defiance
necessary +	ly	= necessarily

When you add a suffix that begins with a vowel to a word that ends in *e*, drop the final *e*. For example:

announce	+	ing	= announcing
continue	+	ous	= continuous

Exceptions are words that end in *–ge* or *–ce*. They keep the final *e* to maintain the soft sound of the *g* or *c*. For example:

| change | + | able | = changeable |
| notice | + | able | = noticeable |

Another exception is

| dye | + | ing | = dyeing |

PRACTICE 7

For each item, add the suffix to the word to make a new word. Use your dictionary to help you.

WORD		SUFFIX	
1. announce	+	ment	=
2. try	+	ing	=
3. happy	+	ness	=
4. associate	+	ion	=
5. dispense	+	able	=
6. definite	+	ly	=
7. accident	+	al	=
8. courage	+	ous	=
9. move	+	able	=
10. hearty	+	ly	=
11. practical	+	ly	=
12. port	+	able	=
13. rude	+	ness	=
14. guide	+	ance	=
15. fulfill	+	ment	=

PRACTICE 8

Circle the number of the incorrectly spelled word in each group. If there is no error, circle number 5.

1. (1) unimportant   (2) revelation   (3) cumulative
   (4) irational   (5) no error

2. (1) brighter   (2) happyness   (3) unaccustomed
   (4) berate   (5) no error

3. (1) impossible   (2) cooperation   (3) inactive
   (4) mispell   (5) no error

4. (1) commencment   (2) coverage   (3) practically
    (4) extraction   (5) no error

5. (1) safty   (2) forgiveness   (3) shining
    (4) amusement   (5) no error

6. (1) becoming   (2) really   (3) plainness
    (4) actually   (5) no error

7. (1) adorable   (2) contagious   (3) acumulate
    (4) supervise   (5) no error

8. (1) loneliness   (2) personal   (3) barely
    (4) noticable   (5) no error

9. (1) continuation   (2) argument   (3) ridiculous
    (4) usage   (5) no error

10. (1) surprised   (2) acquisitiveness   (3) carefully
    (4) virtuous   (5) no error

Stress and Spelling Changes

A word that contains more than one syllable has stress on one of these syllables. For instance, say this word in syllables: *con • cep • tu • al*. One syllable is emphasized. The second. Its stress is marked in this way in a dictionary; *con • cep´ • tu • al*. The stress is on the *cep* syllable. Stress is often a key to spelling.

PRACTICE 9

In each word below, place a stress mark to show which syllable is emphasized. Use a dictionary to help you. The first word is done for you.

1. paint´ • er
2. pri • vate
3. of • fice
4. e • con • o • my
5. ad • vise
6. bal • ance
7. dis • sat • is • fy
8. de • vel • op • ment
9. in • di • vid • u • al
10. pre • fer
11. pref • er • ence
12. psy • chol • o • gy
13. vac • il • late
14. u • nan • i • mous
15. wretch • ed

When you add *–ed* or *–ing* or *–er* to a one-syllable word that ends in a consonant preceded by a vowel, double the final consonant. For example:

plan	planned
set	setting
run	running
thin	thinner

Double the final consonant when you add *–ed, -ing,* or *–ence* to a two-syllable word that ends in a consonant preceded by a vowel *and* whose second syllable is accented. For example:

de • fér	de • férred
oc • cúr	oc • cúrred
oc • cúr	oc • cúr • rence
re • fér	re • fér • ring

When you add *–ence* to a two-syllable word, do *not* double the final consonant if the accent in the new word is *not* on the second syllable. For example:

re • fér	réf • er • ence
con • fér	cón • fer • ence
pre • fér	pré • fer • ence

PRACTICE 10

Circle the number of the incorrectly spelled word in each group. If there is no error, circle number 5.

1. (1) referred (2) preferrence (3) stunning
   (4) winding (5) no error

2. (1) batted (2) conferred (3) reference
   (4) detered (5) no error

3. (1) binder (2) funnier (3) pictured
   (4) reared (5) no error

4. (1) sunning (2) preferable (3) deterent
   (4) banning (5) no error

5. (1) preferred (2) hitting (3) fanned
   (4) occurrence (5) no error

A Spelling Rhyme

Remember this one?

> Use *I* before *e* (*relief*)
> Except after *c* (*receipt*)
> Or when sounding like *a*
> As in *neighbor* or *weigh*.

Other exceptions to this basic rule are *weird, seize, foreign, either, leisure, neither.*

PRACTICE 11

Insert *ei* or *ie* to complete the following words.

1. n_____ce
2. dec_____ve
3. th_____f
4. rel_____ve
5. n_____gh
6. rec_____ve
7. Conc_____ve
8. bel_____f
9. n_____ther
10. s_____ze
11. s_____ge
12. w_____ld

Forming Plurals

These are the rules for forming the plurals of words.

1. Most words form plurals by adding *s*.

pencil	pencils
tree	trees
brochure	brochures
computer	computers

2. Words ending in *y* preceded by a consonant form the plural by changing *y* to *i* and adding *es*.

sky	skies
glory	glories

   Note: If a vowel precedes a final *y*, the plural is formed by adding *s*.

monkey	monkeys
stray	strays

3. Words ending in *o* preceded by a consonant form plurals by adding *es*.

tomato	tomatoes
hero	heroes

Musical words ending in *o* preceded by a consonant usually form the plural by adding only *s*.

alto	altos
piano	pianos

4. Words ending in *s, sh, ch,* and *s* form the plural by adding *es*.

boss	bosses
crush	crushes
porch	porches
tax	taxes

5. A compound word forms its plural by adding *s* to the principal word.

mother-in-law	mothers-in-law
attorney-at-law	attorneys-at-law
mayor-elect	mayors-elect

6. Words ending in *–ful* form the plural by adding *s*.

cupful	cupfuls

7. Some words have the same spelling for the singular and the plural.

one deer	two deer
one trout	two trout
one sheep	two sheep

8. Some words form their plurals by special changes.

thief	thieves
knife	knives
leaf	leaves
woman	women
child	children
tooth	teeth
louse	lice

9. Some words retain their foreign plurals.

crisis	crises
alumnus	alumni
datum	data
appendix	appendices (or appendixes)
bacterium	bacteria
phenomenon	phenomena
criterion	criteria

PRACTICE 12

Circle the number of the incorrectly spelled word in each group. If there is no error, circle number 5. Use your dictionary to help you.

1. (1) geese   (2) mouthsful   (3) commanders-in-chief
    (4) men   (5) no error

2. (1) deers   (2) bases   (3) echoes
    (4) foxes   (5) no error

3. (1) bacilli   (2) son-in-laws   (3) series
    (4) handkerchiefs (5) no error

4. (1) feet   (2) properties   (3) passersby
    (4) mice   (5) no error

5. (1) wolfs   (2) dresses   (3) potatoes
    (4) vice-presidents (5) no error

–Cede, –Ceed, and –Sede

Following are rules regarding the word endings –*sede*, –*ceed*, and –*cede*.

1. Only one word is spelled with a –*sede* ending:

    supersede

2. Only three words are spelled with a –*ceed* ending:

    succeed   exceed   proceed (to go forward)

3. All other words of this type are spelled with a –*cede* ending. For example:

    precede (to go ahead of)   recede   concede

In Summary

As we said at the beginning of this section, spelling correctly comes easily to some people but is achieved only with persistent study by others. For those who need more practice, we have provided many review exercises. You may decide to do only three or four or five of these practices if you see that your score is 90 percent correct or better on each one. If your score is lower, though, you should review the spelling rules and continue with the practices.

These exercises cover a variety of frequently misspelled words. Not every word is covered by a rule given above. If you decide that you need even more help in improving your spelling, study a book that is devoted totally to spelling. We've suggested two titles in the book list on pages XX and XX.

PRACTICE 13

Circle the number of the incorrectly spelled word in each group. If there is no error, circle number 5. Use your dictionary to help you.

1. (1) acknowledge (2) deception (3) conclusivly
   (4) commodity (5) no error

2. (1) incurred (2) apendix (3) voluntary
   (4) herald (5) no error

3. (1) simular (2) bulletin (3) bored
   (4) quizzes (5) no error

4. (1) duchess (2) achevement (3) monarchs
   (4) fertile (5) no error

5. (1) distribute (2) sieze (3) premises
   (4) tonnage (5) no error

6. (1) monthly (2) primarily (3) condemned
   (4) dupped (5) no error

7. (1) cancellation (2) derrick (3) pertinant
   (4) utilize (5) no error

8. (1) nowadays (2) courtesies (3) negotiate
   (4) guardian (5) no error

9. (1) loot (2) faculties (3) lovly
   (4) axle (5) no error

10. (1) fragrance (2) accompanied (3) preference
    (4) athletic (5) no error

PRACTICE 14

Circle the number of the incorrectly spelled word in each group. If there is no error, circle number 5. Use your dictionary to help you.

1. (1) liquid (2) disappear (3) swirling
   (4) dissolve (5) no error

2. (1) inexorable (2) mercyful (3) capacity
   (4) arboreal (5) no error

3. (1) disolution (2) agreeable (3) rammed
   (4) diseases (5) no error

4. (1) minimize (2) sophomore (3) attorneys
   (4) candidacy (5) no error

5. (1) unnecessary   (2) carnage   (3) weird
   (4) judgment   (5) no error

6. (1) roses   (2) government   (3) absence
   (4) churches   (5) no error

7. (1) emergency   (2) eager   (3) cordialy
   (4) citizen   (5) no error

8. (1) benefit   (2) boxes   (3) consequence
   (4) piece   (5) no error

9. (1) journey   (2) majority   (3) necessarily
   (4) relief   (5) no error

10. (1) yacht   (2) traveler   (3) profession
    (4) accede   (5) no error

PRACTICE 15

Circle the number of the incorrectly spelled word in each group. If there is no error, circle number 5. Use your dictionary to help you.

1. (1) overrate   (2) misapprehend   (3) habitualy
   (4) greenness   (5) no error

2. (1) deferred   (2) roping   (3) approval
   (4) applyance   (5) no error

3. (1) candys   (2) valleys   (3) torches
   (4) files   (5) no error

4. (1) immaterial   (2) dissappoint   (3) practically
   (4) unabated   (5) no error

5. (1) embargos   (2) teeth   (3) radios
   (4) sopranos   (5) no error

6. (1) preparing   (2) writing   (3) propeling
   (4) controlled   (5) no error

7. (1) crises   (2) geese   (3) loaves
   (4) trucksful   (5) no error

8. (1) truely   (2) moving   (3) running
   (4) famous   (5) no error

9. (1) shelves   (2) benches   (3) knives
   (4) churches   (5) no error

10. (1) salarys   (2) basketfuls   (3) reddest
    (4) nameless   (5) no error

PRACTICE 16

Circle the incorrectly spelled word in each group. If there is no error, circle number 5. Use your dictionary to help you.

1. (1) belief   (2) achieve   (3) neice
   (4) weigh   (5) no error

2. (1) yield   (2) neighbor   (3) deceive
   (4) releif   (5) no error

3. (1) benefited   (2) appealed   (3) refered
   (4) equipped   (5) no error

4. (1) preference   (2) reference   (3) asessment
   (4) colonel   (5) no error

5. (1) motivating   (2) humorous   (3) sophomore
   (4) similar   (5) no error

6. (1) primarily   (2) adjustment   (3) preoccupy
   (4) receit   (5) no error

7. (1) acquired   (2) brief   (3) contemptible
   (4) height   (5) no error

8. (1) erred   (2) millionaire (3) potatoes
   (4) lieutenant   (5) no error

9. (1) adjournament (2) caucus   (3) contagious
   (4) digestible   (5) no error

10. (1) carefuly   (2) calendar   (3) macaroni
    (4) preceding   (5) no error

PRACTICE 17

Circle the number of the incorrectly spelled word in each group. If there is no error, circle number 5. Use your dictionary to help you.

1. (1) changeable   (2) athletetic   (3) grammar
   (4) fortissimo   (5) no error

2. (1) filial   (2) leisure   (3) temperture
   (4) treachery   (5) no error

3. (1) bulletin   (2) amendment   (3) incessent
   (4) kindergarten (5) no error

4. (1) legitiment   (2) persuade   (3) pervade
   (4) courtesies   (5) no error

5. (1) prefer   (2) preferred   (3) preference
    (4) patrolled   (5) no error

6. (1) ninth   (2) correspondent   (3) canoe
    (4) hideous   (5) no error

7. (1) apparently   (2) foreign   (3) carriage
    (4) forfeit   (5) no error

8. (1) aggregate   (2) massacre   (3) omissions
    (4) tetnus   (5) no error

9. (1) exceed   (2) intercede   (3) proceed
    (4) procedure   (5) no error

10. (1) fundimental   (2) misspell   (3) hypocrite
    (4) penitentiary   (5) no error

PRACTICE 18

Circle the number of the incorrectly spelled word in each group. If there is no error, circle number 5. Use your dictionary to help you.

1. (1) torches   (2) salaries   (3) valleys
    (4) shelves   (5) no error

2. (1) absense   (2) gases   (3) accident
    (4) capitalize   (5) no error

3. (1) executive   (2) divide   (3) discusion
    (4) eager   (5) no error

4. (1) contrary   (2) atheletic   (3) critical
    (4) banquet   (5) no error

5. (1) association   (2) character   (3) earliest
    (4) decide   (5) no error

6. (1) Wenesday   (2) knives   (3) concerning
    (4) communicate   (5) no error

7. (1) appreciate   (2) except   (3) scene
    (4) numerous   (5) no error

8. (1) national   (2) posession   (3) industrious
    (4) volume   (5) no error

9. (1) patient   (2) quantity   (3) boundary
    (4) probably   (5) no error

10. (1) warrant   (2) laboratory   (3) interesting
    (4) libary   (5) no error

PRACTICE 19

Circle the number of the incorrectly spelled word in each group. If there is no error, circle number 5. Use your dictionary to help you.

1. (1) biased   (2) aberation   (3) wholly
    (4) vacuum   (5) no error

2. (2) sensible   (2) ecstasy   (3) embarrass
    (4) essential   (5) no error

3. (1) asertain   (2) correlation (3) abeyance
    (4) diocese   (5) no error

4. (1) fifth   (2) resileince   (3) nickel
    (4) official   (5) no error

5. (1) satellite   (2) originate   (3) illegitimate
    (4) policy   (5) no error

6. (1) subversive (2) predatory   (3) lucritive
    (4) prairie   (5) no error

7. (1) pacifist   (2) senior   (3) source
    (4) wheather   (5) no error

8. (1) weild   (2) vacillate   (3) vengeance
    (4) transaction (5) no error

9. (1) queue   (2) masquerade   (3) preside
    (4) prohibit   (5) no error

10. (1) psicology   (2) possession   (3) measurable
    (4) impeccable (5) no error

PRACTICE 20

Circle the number of the incorrectly spelled word in each group. If there is no error, circle number 5. Use your dictionary to help you.

1. (1) derogatory (2) neglagible   (3) rehearsal
    (4) yacht   (5) no error

2. (1) peculiar   (2) jeopardy   (3) forfiet
    (4) respondent (5) no error

3. (1) bureau   (2) blamable   (3) desecration
    (4) harass   (5) no error

4. (1) falibility (2) heinous   (3) myriad
    (4) remnant   (5) no error

5. (1) hygienic   (2) medallion   (3) midget
    (4) prommisory   (5) no error

6. (1) complacency   (2) ephemeral   (3) exagerate
    (4) realize   (5) no error

7. (1) lacquer   (2) currency   (3) exortation
    (4) harassment   (5) no error

8. (1) apologetic   (2) coroner   (3) clique
    (4) exzema   (5) no error

9. (1) disatisfied   (2) moribund   (3) warrant
    (4) surgeon   (5) no error

10. (1) defered   (2) extraordinary   (3) journal
    (4) intercede   (5) no error

ANSWERS

PRACTICE 1

1. Before leaving the office, Mr. Tevis reviewed all of the day's cases.
2. He and I work for the same company, and we take the train together.
3. C
4. It isn't that we don't want to join you; we just can't.
5. "If I had known you were serving dinner," said Isabel, "I would not have eaten earlier."
6. Martin Haber, my ex-boss, was at the dinner.
7. When you arrive at the airport in Seattle, Washington, please give me a call.
8. Gregory Tesides, the Symphony Club president, and his wife, a librarian, chaired the benefit for the local hospital.

PRACTICE 2

1. The word processor can identify all the number 6's in the report.
2. While many people were concerned about minor pollutants such as solid waste, the more serious problem of toxic waste surfaced.
3. "College costs have risen to an all-time high," said Chancellor Mendoza.
4. Motivation is not enough; you must earn better grades.
5. Although Clara had expected some problems, her new job as the dean's assistant is challenging and rewarding.
6. That woman—the one in the yellow dress—is Sarah's mother. [**or** That woman (the one in the yellow dress) is Sarah's mother.]
7. Jake isn't working tonight, but Keith will substitute for him.
8. Did you read the article about self-styled nutrition experts?
9. When you are in Lincoln, Nebraska, you can visit a friend of mine.
10. Chuck Hardwick, our local assemblyman, is a very responsive and responsible legislator.
11. Some legislators, however, respond to mail only with form letters.
12. The shipment did arrive on time; however, several items we had ordered were not included.
13. I won't ask you again; forget it.
14. If you thought thirty-nine was a difficult birthday, wait until you are forty-nine.
15. Our department can't run effectively without the following supplies: file folders, address labels, envelopes, pencils, a pencil sharpener, and felt-tip pens.

PRACTICE 3

July 12, 2000

Ms. Hilda Blume
Wilson Supply Company
419 West Broad Street
Westfield, New Jersey 07090

Dear Ms. Blume:

Since you and I spoke on June 24, I have decided to give our office supply order to your company. I assume that the terms we discussed during that conversation still apply.

Instead of waiting for your official order form, I will place our order now. Please send us the following items:
> 3 reams of 20 lb. paper
> 6 dozen pencils (number 2's)
> 1 box of Smith's Erasable Bond

Thank you for your immediate attention to this order.

I look forward to our working together. By the way, the next time you are in our part of town with samples, please call me.

Sincerely,
Mary Ellen Collins

PRACTICE 4

1. Our company, Ralme, Inc., moved its headquarters to Carson City, Nevada, in the spring of 1982.
2. We've asked Mr. Arthur Ralme to chair the Board of Directors of Hewes Corporation.
3. After we leave San Francisco, we'll travel in the Orient for two weeks.
4. Submit your bid to the Department of Transportation, Washington, D.C.
5. First walk east on Main Street until you reach East Fourth Avenue.
6. Have you read the new book on management, *Making Time Make You Money?*

PRACTICE 5

1. Answer each call as quickly as possible.
2. Determine that the caller is a member.
   a. Ask the caller for his/her name and address.
   b. Insert facts into the computer.
   c. Ask the caller for his/her membership number and expiration date.
   d. Check these details with the computer printout.
3. Take the order. Enter the order into the computer.
4. Repeat the order to the customer.
   These instructions take effect on February 1.

PRACTICE 6
January 10, 2001

Mr. Lorenzo Mendoza
67 Main Street
Wilmington, Delaware 19823

Dear Mr. Mendoza:

We are happy to confirm your family's reservations for February 22–26, and are delighted to welcome you again this year. You requested two rooms on the second floor, which we will reserve for you.

Since last year, we've added many winter sports activities. I'm sending you our new brochure, which describes these activities. I know that your family, in particular, will enjoy the night skiing.

If I can do anything else to help you plan your vacation, please let me know.

Sincerely,

Marge Browning

PRACTICE 7
1. announcement
2. trying
3. happiness
4. association
5. dispensable
6. definitely
7. accidental
8. courageous
9. movable
10. heartily
11. practically
12. portable
13. rudeness
14. guidance
15. fulfillment

PRACTICE 8
1. (4) irrational
2. (2) happiness
3. (4) misspell
4. (1) commencement
5. (1) safety
6. (5) No error
7. (3) accumulate
8. (4) noticeable

9.   (2) argument
10. (5) No error

PRACTICE 9

1.   paint´ • er
2.   pri´ • vate
3.   of´ • fice
4.   e • con´ • o • my
5.   ad • vise´
6.   bal´• ance
7.   dis • sat´ • is • fy
8.   de • vel´ • op • ment
9.   in • di • vid´ • u • al
10. pre • fer´
11. pref´ • er • ence
12. psy • chol´ • o • gy
13. vac´ • il late
14. u • nan´ • i • mous
15. wretch´ • ed

PRACTICE 10

1.   (2) preference
2.   (4) deterred
3.   (5) No error
4.   (3) deterrent
5.   (4) occurrence

PRACTICE 11

1.   niece
2.   deceive
3.   thief
4.   relieve
5.   neigh
6.   receive
7.   conceive
8.   belief
9.   neither
10. seize
11. siege
12. wield

PRACTICE 12

1.   (2) mouthfuls
2.   (1) deer
3.   (2) sons-in-law
4.   (5) No error
5.   (1) wolves

PRACTICE 13
1.   (3) conclusively
2.   (2) appendix
3.   (1) similar
4.   (2) achievement
5.   (2) seize
6.   (4) duped
7.   (3) pertinent
8.   (5) No error
9.   (3) lovely
10. (5) No error

PRACTICE 14
1.   (5) No error
2.   (2) merciful
3.   (1) dissolution
4.   (5) No error
5.   (3) weird
6.   (2) government
7.   (3) cordially
8.   (4) piece
9.   (5) No error
10. (5) No error

PRACTICE 15
1.   (3) habitually
2.   (4) appliance
3.   (1) candies
4.   (2) disappoint
5.   (1) embargoes
6.   (3) propelling
7.   (4) truckfuls
8.   (1) truly
9.   (5) No error
10. (1) salaries

PRACTICE 16
1.   (3) niece
2.   (4) relief
3.   (3) referred
4.   (3) assessment
5.   (5) No error
6.   (4) receipt
7.   (1) acquired
8.   (4) lieutenant
9.   (1) adjournment
10. (1) carefully

PRACTICE 17

1. (2) athletic
2. (3) temperature
3. (3) incessant
4. (1) legitimate
5. (5) No error
6. (5) No error
7. (5) No error
8. (4) tetanus
9. (5) No error
10. (1) fundamental

PRACTICE 18

1. (5) No error
2. (1) absence
3. (3) discussion
4. (2) athletic
5. (5) No error
6. (1) Wednesday
7. (5) No error
8. (2) possession
9. (5) No error
10. (4) library

PRACTICE 19

1. (2) aberration
2. (5) No error
3. (1) ascertain
4. (2) resilience
5. (5) No error
6. (3) lucrative
7. (4) weather/whether
8. (1) wield
9. (5) No error
10. (1) psychology

PRACTICE 20

1. (2) negligible
2. (3) forfeit
3. (5) No error
4. (1) fallibility
5. (4) promissory
6. (3) exaggerate
7. (3) exhortation
8. (4) eczema
9. (1) dissatisfied
10. (1) deferred

10.

Develop Your Vocabulary _____

If you find when you sit down to write that words don't come readily, take heart. You are not alone in this problem. Many people have difficulty finding the right words to express their thoughts. The more words you have at your command, the more easily they will flow. General vocabulary development is an asset to anyone. Specific vocabulary development will help you with your particular writing needs.

General Vocabulary Development

You may have heard it before, but this technique *is* valuable. Carry a small notebook with you. When you hear or read an unfamiliar word, jot it down. When you have time, look up the definition in the dictionary. If you are very ambitious, you can also look the word up in a thesaurus, or dictionary of synonyms. You may encounter synonyms you are already familiar with; knowing these words should make it easier for you to learn the new word.

But keeping a notebook of words and definitions will increase your vocabulary only minimally—unless you *use* the new words. In order to truly *own* a new vocabulary word, you must use it correctly. You may feel uncomfortable at first. It is interesting to note that few people are embarrassed to display a limited vocabulary. Many of us, however, are uncomfortable about appearing too smart. We don't want to offend others or to seem arrogant. Consequently, when we *can* say, "They *ostracize* people who disagree with their politics," we might instead choose, "They shut out people who disagree with their politics." Get used to using your new words. Wear them proudly.

Specific Vocabulary Development

In addition to enlarging your general vocabulary, you should learn words that will help you with your personal writing needs. If you are a student, you need the broadest possible vocabulary in each field of study. Try the same techniques you used to collect general vocabulary: collect, define, use, and review. The texts and other books you read and the lectures and discussions you hear are all sources of new vocabulary.

Or perhaps, as a laboratory technician, you have to prepare monthly reports or write up the results of your experiments. If so, concentrate on learning the words and phrases that will help you explain your findings clearly and accurately. Be sure to keep your audience in mind. Are your readers fellow scientists or a lay advisory board? Remember to develop and use a vocabulary that your audience will understand.

Are you responsible for writing grants or proposals? Learn the acceptable, appropriate terminology.

Most businesses, professions, and school subjects have their own jargons, their own special vocabularies. Jargon has a specific meaning and, in fact, makes sense only in a particular context. Used properly, this special vocabulary is acceptable. Certain words, however, seem to hold a particular attraction for many people who use them in the wrong context. For example, you hear and see the word *interface,* which has a particular meaning in computer technology, misused regularly. An *interface* is a thing (a noun), an electrical gadget. Yet, it is used regularly in other contexts.

> Correct: Use a serial *interface* to connect the printer to your computer.
> Incorrect: The two committees will *interface* (meet) to compare their plans.

As you increase your vocabulary, therefore, remember to use special words in their proper places. A complete dictionary helps you do that by listing all the ways a word is defined. In addition, some dictionaries provide usage notes that discuss acceptable usage.

Using the Dictionary

How often, when reading a novel, a magazine, a textbook, or even a letter, have you come across an unfamiliar word? Do you skip over it as though it never existed? Tell yourself you'll get back to it later and look it up? Write it down and plan to look it up? Or actually look it up?

Let us say you actually do look up the definition of the new word. Do you then assume you'll remember it? Write it down to assist your memory? Write it down and occasionally review it? Or write it down, review it, and use it?

To help you develop a technique for expanding your vocabulary, try the following exercises.

PRACTICE 1

For each word below, do the following:

1. Look the word up in the dictionary and select one meaning, preferably the most common.

2. Write the dictionary definition of the word.

3. Write at least one synonym. Use a thesaurus if necessary.

4. Use the word in a sentence.

vanguard	emulate	sedulous
articulate	ineluctable	gratuitous
entrench	sanctimonious	penurious
debility	coveted	indictment

User-Friendly and Unfriendly Definitions

Learning to get the most from your dictionary takes practice. For instance, sometimes a dictionary defines a word by giving another form of the word itself. For example:

intensity   the quality or condition of being *intense.*

Chances are, if you knew what *intense* meant, you would have been able to figure out what *intensity* meant. Often, of course, the dictionary will also provide more helpful definitions, such as *energy, strength, concentration* for *intensity.* But what if it doesn't? Then you'll have to look up the other form of the word—in this case, *intense.*

For most words, the dictionary offers more than one definition. Make certain that you select the definition that suits your use of the word. The dictionary also identifies parts of speech. It is helpful to know whether the word you want to use is a noun, a verb, an adjective, or an adverb. For example, you would not write "Theo looked intense (*adj.*) at Amanda." Correct usage would be "Theo looked intensely (*adv.*) at Amanda."

As you can see, most new words you learn come with a family. Consider your vocabulary development similar to shopping at a sale: buy one, get two or three for free! Once you learn *intense,* for instance, you'll understand the meaning of *intensely, intensity*, and *intensive.* Now that's a bargain!

PRACTICE 2

Select the correct word for each sentence below.

intense   intensely   intensive   intensity

1.   The _____ glare from the headlights made driving difficult.

2.   Chas works with such _____ that others have trouble working with him.

3.   As a result of _____ research, I found the exact information I needed.

4.   The state trooper pursued the hit-and-run driver _____.

PRACTICE 3

Write your own sentences using the above forms of *intense.*

_____

_____

_____

_____

PRACTICE 4

Select one of the following words to complete each sentence below.

extreme   extremist   extremities

1. Wear warm socks and gloves on your _____, or you'll get frostbite.

2. Tearing one's hair out is an _____ example of frustration.

3. Seen as an _____ in his isolationist beliefs, the senator was shunned.

Using Context Clues

Have you noticed that people who read a great deal tend to have larger vocabularies? Reading gives you the opportunity to increase your vocabulary because often the words you don't know are surrounded by others you *do* know. The words and phrases that surround a word are called the *context*. Suppose, as you read the following paragraph, you don't know the meaning of the word *retain*. What context clues can help you unlock the meaning of this word?

> All matter can be broken down into smaller units. The molecule is the smallest unit of matter that can exist independently and *retain* its chemical properties. Once a molecule is broken into smaller particles, or atoms, the chemical properties of the original substance do not necessarily remain.

After reading the passage, which of these words do you think is the correct definition of *retain:* (1) change; (2) destroy; (3) keep; (4) lose; (5) break? You decide that the correct answer is number 3, keep. How did you reach that conclusion? Perhaps your thinking went like this: The paragraph says that a molecule is the smallest unit that can *retain* its chemical properties, or characteristics. On the other hand, if a molecule is broken down, these properties do not necessarily remain. This sentence suggests that, until the molecule breaks down, it does *keep,* or *retain,* its chemical properties. Thus you can guess that *retain* means "keep."

PRACTICE 5

Use context clues to help you select the correct definition for the italicized word in each paragraph.

1. In recent years, there has been a great emphasis on the high-technology professions. Numerous students have been trained for these positions, usually considered the "wave of the future." Some educators are concerned, however, that the tide will run out before those students currently riding the wave reach the shore—or the job market. Several decades ago the trend in education was to counsel most students to become teachers. During the 1960s, there was a *glut* on the market, and many trained teachers were forced to seek other fields of employment. Will the new millenium bring a glut of people trained to work in high-tech fields? *Glut* means (1) employment; (2) economy; (3) excess; (4) earnings; (5) demand.

2. The public has become increasingly aware of the dangers *posed* by chemical waste. At one time, no one questioned an industry's right to manufacture products and to dispose of wastes as it saw fit. Today, just as nonsmokers demand "breathing space" from smokers, many citizens are holding neighboring industries responsible for keeping the air and water clean.
    In the above paragraph, *posed* means (1) modeled; (2) asked; (3) presented; (4) hidden; (5) covered up.

3. Work is the salvation of some and the *bane* of others. While scores of people scurry to their offices eager for the day's work, just as many reluctantly trudge to work as though going to jail. The right kind of job can provide satisfaction. Sometimes, though, we require an incentive beyond the job itself, an incentive such as the need to support a family or to pay for our education.

Bane means (1) savings; (2) love; (3) reluctance; (4) motivation; (5) curse.

Using Word Parts

Finally, you can improve your vocabulary by examining the structure of words to see how they are formed. The main part of a word is called the *root* (for instance, *write*). To that we can add prefixes to the beginning (*re*write) and suffixes to the end (writ*er*). By learning common roots, prefixes, and suffixes, you can increase your understanding of the meanings of words. Many roots are taken from Latin and Greek words. Review these common prefixes:

Prefix	Meaning	Usage
pre-	before	This manuscript predates the Bible.
in-	not	The work is still incomplete.
im-	not	It will be impossible to finish it on time.
dis-	not	Many people dislike working overtime.
ex-	out of	Excommunication is a severe penalty.
un-	not	Right now, earning a Ph.D. is an unrealistic goal.
a-	outside of, not	January's low productivity was atypical for our firm.
auto-	self, same	Have you read Margaret Mead's autobiography?
re-	again	The new tenant wants us to redesign the first floor.
mal-	bad	One more malfunction and I am getting rid of this computer!
il-	not	A major problem in our society is illiteracy.
ir-	not	These blouses are inexpensive because they are irregular.
co-	with	Marisol has requested our cooperation.
mis-	wrong	The child was scolded for misbehavior.

Now here are some common suffixes:

Suffix	Meaning	Usage
-ness	state of	Cliff expressed happi<u>ness</u> at his promotion.
-ly	every, like	Please review these hour<u>ly</u> reports carefully.
-ous	full of, having	If this product is successful, we could become fam<u>ous</u>.
-able	capable of	I find Mr. Coste's offer reason<u>able</u>.
-ive	forms adjectives or nouns from verbs	Gabrielle is our most creat<u>ive</u> writer.
-ance	forms nouns from verbs or adjectives	After your injury, I understand your reluct<u>ance</u> to play on the company team.
-ment	result or state	This establish<u>ment</u> has a fine reputation.
-ion	state or condition	Airfares have declined since deregulat<u>ion</u>.
-al	pertaining to	Dr. Wilenski does not consider this a practic<u>al</u> move.
-ful	characterized by	Please be tact<u>ful</u> when you refuse his help.
-er	doer	This plant hired another weld<u>er</u>.
-or	doer	Doris is the creat<u>or</u> of these sculptures.

And here are some helpful root words:

Root	Origin	Meaning	Usage
tekne	Greek	skill	<u>technology</u>: You can't always transfer the newest scientific *technology* to a commercial product.
alere	Latin	to nourish	<u>alimentary</u>: In the digestive process, food passes through the *alimentary* canal.
putare	Latin	to think	<u>compute</u>: The flowchart describes how we *compute* the average of the class's grades.
videre	Latin	to see	<u>video</u>: Are you comfortable looking at a *video* display screen?
dominium	Latin	property	<u>domicile</u>: Include your *domicile,* or legal residence, on that form.
bene	Latin	well	<u>benefit</u>: The program will *benefit* my favorite charity.
dicere	Latin	to say	<u>dictate</u>: The office manager would always *dictate* his letters and memos in the afternoon, when the office was quieter.
facere	Latin	to do, make	<u>factory</u>: The company assembles the product at their newest *factory.*
volens	Latin	wishing	<u>voluntary</u>: Supposedly, attending the meeting was *voluntary.*
unus	Latin	one, single	<u>unite</u>: Our common goals for the company *unite* us.
signum	Latin	sign	<u>signal</u>: The flashing light we saw was a *signal* of the ship's arrival.
portare	Latin	to carry	<u>portable</u>: I don't intend missing the game; I'm going to take a *portable* television set with me.
manu	Latin	by hand	<u>manual</u>: On that machine, *manual* mode means that the operator must turn it on and off.
ferre	Latin	to bear, carry	<u>transfer</u>: Mildred Jackson accepted a *transfer* to the Chicago office.
ducere	Latin	to lead	<u>ducts</u>: The exocrine glands discharge their fluids through *ducts.*
scribere	Latin	to write	<u>scribble</u>: Because we have a word processor now, you won't have to interpret what I *scribble.*

PRACTICE 6

From the list below, add to each of the words in the exercise a prefix that will form a new word.

in-   re-   ir-   ac-   de-   co-
mal-   im-   mis-   un-   dis-   il-

1. _____nutrition
2. _____education
3. _____appropriate
4. _____reverent
5. _____patient
6. _____legal

7. _____inform
8. _____available
9. _____assemble
10. _____pay
11. _____personalize
12. _____climate

PRACTICE 7

Complete the following sentences by adding a prefix or suffix to the italicized word in each. In some cases, you will have to make minor spelling changes.

1. The sudden appearance of the dark shadow *mobilized* the frightened child.

2. Because the testimony was *relevant,* the judge ordered it stricken from the record.

3. If you are always complaining, you will earn the title of office *content.*

4. You must understand my *ease* at competing with you for this position.

5. While supplies are *plenty* , I don't mind lending them to other departments.

6. Even Agatha Christie would not have *covered* the cause of that fire.

7. Unless we invest in *educate* , our entire society will lose.

8. John has a record of all deposits, but no record of the *disburse* of funds.

9. I give up; I find this problem *solvable.*

10. A committee of interested citizens decided to *store* the town hall that had been built in 1805.

ANSWERS

PRACTICE 1

These sentences are suggestions, of course. Your sentences will differ, but make sure your usage is correct.

vanguard (forefront)	the foremost position in an army, fleet, or movement (n). Gloria Steinem has always been in the *vanguard* of the women's movement.
articulate (eloquent-adj. say-v.)	able to speak clearly and eloquently (adj.) To speak clearly; to express ideas well (v.) William is the most *articulate* speaker on the debating team. If you can't *articulate* what you mean, your listeners may find your ideas confusing.
entrench (establish)	to fix securely, to establish (v.) The squirrels are firmly *entrenched* in our attic.
debility (weakness)	weakness, infirmity (n.) Dr. Garcia's *debility* forced him to retire at age fifty.
emulate (copy)	to try to equal or exceed; to imitate (v.) Martin Luther King, Jr. was a great leader whom young people would do well to *emulate*.
ineluctable (inevitable)	not to be avoided or overcome; inevitable (adj.) Although we knew what to expect, we watched the soap opera to learn the *ineluctable* fate of the heroine.
sanctimonious (hypocritical)	pretending to be righteous; hypocritical (adj.) *Sanctimonious* political candidates may make moving speeches calling for aid to the needy and then do nothing for them after the election.
coveted (desirable)	highly desirable or sought after (adj.) The Olympic athletes competed for the *coveted* medals.
sedulous (diligent)	diligent, persevering (adj.) Although John seemed to be a *sedulous* student, his grades did not reflect much effort.
gratuitous (free)	unearned, free, unwarranted (adj.) Don gives *gratuitous* advice to people who cannot afford to pay a lawyer.
penurious (miserly)	extremely stingy, miserly, penny-pinching (adj.) The old man was so *penurious* that he refused to buy proper food for himself or his dog.
indictment (disapproval)	accusation, charges (n.) The supervisor's critical memo was clearly an *indictment* of the assistant's behavior.

PRACTICE 2

1. The *intense* glare from the headlights made driving difficult.
2. Phil works with such *intensity* that others have trouble working with him.
3. As a result of *intensive* research, I found the exact information I needed.
4. The state trooper pursued the hit-and-run driver *intensely*.

PRACTICE 3

Answers will vary.

PRACTICE 4

1. Wear warm socks and gloves on your *extremities,* or you'll get frostbite.
2. Tearing one's hair out is an *extreme* example of frustration.
3. Seen as an *extremist* in his isolationist beliefs, the senator was shunned.

PRACTICE 5

1. (3) excess
2. (3) presented
3. (5) curse

PRACTICE 6

1. malnutrition
2. coeducation
3. inappropriate (*or* misappropriate)
4. irreverent
5. impatient
6. illegal
7. misinform
8. unavailable
9. disassemble (*or* reassemble)
10. repay
11. depersonalize (*or* impersonalize)
12. acclimate

PRACTICE 7

1. immobilized
2. irrelevant
3. malcontent
4. unease
5. plentiful
6. uncovered *or* discovered
7. education
8. disbursement
9. unsolvable *or* insolvable
10. restore

11.

Edit and Rewrite _____

You've finished the first draft of your report or letter. You followed our suggestions and wrote the draft as quickly as possible. You didn't get bogged down looking for the precise word or writing the perfect sentence or paragraph. No, you just whizzed ahead, following your plan, and left plenty of room for corrections and additions. Then you put your writing aside for a day or more to become objective and develop a keener eye for errors. Now, you're ready to get back to work. Get out your red pencil.

   The editing and rewriting you'll do now, although not the final step, is one of the most important stages in revision. Experts say that you will probably find 75 to 80 percent of your errors in this first reading.

Editing the First Draft

As you begin editing, ask yourself some important questions. Did you:

1. FOLLOW A PLAN? Does your letter, memo, or report follow your original plan? Perhaps you did follow your plan but now find that the ideas could be arranged more effectively. Move those misplaced sentences or paragraphs. Don't hesitate to change the order of ideas. On second look, you may find a better way of saying what you want to get across to the reader.
2. ACCOMPLISH YOUR PURPOSE? Have you accomplished your purpose? Look at the purpose statement you wrote when you first began to plan your memo, letter, report, or essay (see Chapter 1). Have you accomplished what you set out to do: inform, request, persuade, motivate, or entertain?
3. USE SUPPORTING IDEAS? Are your ideas well supported? You may need to expand on an idea and add evidence to your argument. On the other hand, if you've gone beyond the subject matter in defending a point, you may need to shorten that paragraph or delete an entire section.
4. ACHIEVE THE RIGHT TONE? Is the tone of your writing appropriate? Some people answer this question by reading their writing aloud. You can read to a friend—real or imagined—and ask yourself along the way, "Is this the way I would talk?" "Is my idea stated in a conversational way?" "Is the letter overwritten and stiff?"
5. CHOOSE THE MOST PRECISE WORDS? Have you chosen the correct, the most precise words and avoided gobbledygook that stifles understanding?
6. WRITE CORRECT SENTENCES? Correct any run-on sentences and sentence fragments. Check that ideas are properly listed. Did you use verbs and pronouns correctly? Are modifiers placed near the words they describe?

7. USE CORRECT SPELLING, PUNCTUATION, AND CAPITALIZATION? Are the mechanics in order? Even minor errors can detract from the quality of your letter, memo, or report.

Proofreading, a Necessary Skill

Proofreading must be done in several steps:

1. **Read through for content.**
    *   Do not expect to pick up errors in grammar, spelling, and punctuation.
    *   Look for missing or transposed words or sentences.
    *   Look for errors in information.
2. **Read for grammar, spelling, and punctuation.**
    *   Point, if you must, to force yourself to read each word.
    *   Read backwards to check for spelling errors only.
3. **Read one more time to ensure that changes did not alter consistency.**
    *   Make certain that a change in the first paragraph is consistent with later copy.
4. **Have another person proofread your work.**
    *   A fresh set of eyes is helpful.

PRACTICE 1

Correct the word usage errors in the following sentences.
Note: Every sentence has an error.

1. Please except my apology.
2. Jim doesn't want to argue. He said to leave it be.
3. Ms. Atler did not intend her comments to infer that you were incompetent.
4. Please carry your résumé to the Personal Department.
5. Any good report clearly states the principle issues.
6. Salad and fresh bread make a healthy lunch.
7. When Mr. Shen wants your advise, he will certainly ask for it.
8. When I have time for a break, I will lay down for a few minutes.
9. You sure don't think that I could type that quickly, do you?
10. This is a whole nother topic.
11. I found last year's seminar more valuable then this year's.
12. Mr. Salle came in the meeting room 45 minutes late.
13. The choice for best composition is between these four.
14. There are less people in line for the 6:40 show than there are for the 8:40.

15. Many people are becoming concerned about the affects of air pollution on our health.

16. Ira is anxious to see the new play.

17. José cannot find that position paper anywheres.

18. Its not too late to cancel the plane reservations.

PRACTICE 2

Edit these paragraphs. Look for errors in grammar, punctuation, spelling, capitalization, word usage, and sentence structure. Then check your answers against the answer key at the end of the chapter.

1. During the past century, chemistry has been involved in playing a part in the studying of the life sciences. As a result of this, there has been, increasingly, a coming together of the research going on in chemistry with the other sciences. Increasing knowledge as far as comlex chemical structures are concerned, is helping scientists to under basic life processes. This is the area of biochemistry—a bringing together of biology and chemistry.

2. At our last meeting you asked for my insight as to building your new plant in Clayton. First and utmost is the financial dividends your company would receive. By locating their the corporate tax rate in Clayton is the lowest in the state. Also you will have no trouble relocating employees to the area, everyone knows it as a fine town in which anyone can live.

3. Here is an account of the Texas controversy. In the Louisiana purchase of 1803, the U.S. obtained the title to Texas from France, which they later passed on to Spain in the Adams-Onis Agreement of 1819 in return for Florida. In the same year, Moses Austin was granted a grant of land from Spain to settle a colony in Texas. His son, under a newly created Mexican government, independent of Spain, established a colony between the Brazos and Colorado rivers.

4. Public Relations Announcement
The company's supervisor of operations states, "if a customer has a problem relative to our machinery, I get the call direct. With our direct contact with our representatives all over the Country, I can make the necessary delivery and repairing is also a possibility. Our salespeople are like family. There just as anxious to affect the needed change as we are. Customers appreciate that.

5. Sometimes personal learning needs are not met by existing curriculum. So independent study can be another facet of the Adult College Plan. This gives the student an option. That is to create a study program tailored to their needs.

Classes are held in the evening. That way students are still able to work at their jobs during the day. They also can use their work as a laboratory. Here they blend theory and practice under supervision. They also earn credit for it.

PRACTICE 3

Edit the following essay for errors in grammar, punctuation, capitalization, and word usage. Also, consider the order in which ideas are presented. Then, check your answers against the answer key at the end of the chapter.

I have a stack of ads that I cut out, glued to index cards, and in response to which I have called or sent my résumé. Usually, the eye-catching ads that offer the most highest starting salaries involves sales work. That's not, however, something I enjoy doing. As I learned in High School.

One job I really wanted was a manager trainee in a bookstore. Part of the interview entailed a 30-page questionnaire. Question topics included corruption and drug abuse; employee theft; possible criminal record of applicant; and, my personal favorite, "Do you have any bad habits?" I had to say no. Sometimes, I wonder if having bad habits would have gotten me the job.

PRACTICE 4

Change the tone of the following letter by replacing the italicized words with words from the list below. You will have to change *a* to *an* in one case.

inferior	received	recently	quality
extremely	request	appear	

249 Lenox Avenue
Cranford, New Jersey 07076
March 7, 2000

Mr. John Railier, President
World Wide Distributors
400 North Avenue
Westfield, New Jersey 07090

Dear Mr. Rainier:

I *just got* your package and must say I was *very* disappointed. You had promised me a *good* product, and I received a *junky* one. How can such a well-known company *come off* to be reputable and yet make such an unreliable item? I respectfully *ask for* a refund.

Sincerely,
Ben Zmuda

PRACTICE 5

Rewrite the following letters correctly. There are errors in form, grammar, capitalization, spelling, and punctuation.

LETTER 1

Martin Rivera
Well-Built Construction Company
21 Warren Road
San Francisco, CA 90042

Dear Mr. Rivera,

You were highly recommended by my neighbor but I fail to see why. A three-day project ends up taking two Weeks. Your workmen left my yard a shambles after building a garage for me. I ask the men to clean up their garbage but they refused. Please have someone from well-built complete this cleanup within the next five days. Thank-you.

sincerely,
Wilma Jones
San Francisco, CA 90042

LETTER 2

April 2, 2000
Mr. Melvin Appley
27 Main Street
Smalltown, USA 00000

Arthur Johnson
Superintendent of Schools
110 Pine Street
Smalltown, PA 10001

Dear Superintendent Johnson,

I would like to take this opportunity to say that I am in receipt of and have read your report on raising eligibility standards for high school athltes which you reported to our school. My argument against higher academic standards for athltes centers around the fact that a student can pass from grade to grade with a 1.5 average but they can't play football. Hows that fair?

I'm not saying that it's not true that the first job of any student in school should be academic. I'm just saying you can't say "that no one without a 3.0 average can participate in sports." That doesn't take into account special students needs or abilities. Also, a students' educational experience should be as complete as possible, it should include the interaction that takes place in sports. Please consider your position in this matter.

Sincerely,
Melvin Appley

LETTER 3

GILBEY CONSTRUCTION COMPANY
180 Main Street   Westfield, Kansas 66614

Mr. Steven Perl, president
Perfect Product Co.
Lubbock, Texas 79403

Dear Steve:

I am in receipt of your product brochure which explains all the data on your partitions. We found it very informative and most likely is the product we are in need of. A few questions still remain unanswered. The particular modle we are looking for must be able to be mounted directly to a ceramic floor. Can this be done? Since we have limited space what is the required space that your product needs? Our client has asked us to pursue this product made of PVC in a peach color. Is it available and if so what would be your quickest delivery time? Please fax your responses as soon as possible along with any warranty information you might have.

Sincerely
Martin Morez

PRACTICE 6

Rewrite the following memos correctly. There are errors in form, grammar, capitalization, spelling, and punctuation.

MEMO 1
FROM: Chaya Cohen
TO: Laura Perez

About our 2002 annual sales conference. Im assembling my presentation to the sales representatives but I find I'll need some audio-visuals—can you get me a large screen, slide projector, and a lighted pointer. Also, the sound system at last years Conference is inadequate for the size room we had. Will you be able to improve on that this time?
Let's meat about 2 week's before the conference and go over the points I'll be covering, in case you have some particular products you want covering in depth.

MEMO 2
TO: All Department Heads
FROM: Bill Morrisey
DATE: January 12, 2001
SUBJECT: Weekly progress reports

As you all know, each and every Monday morning I meet with Mr. Smith and Mr. Torres. At these meetings I have to give a weekly progress report of all our departments. Without your reports by Friday it makes for a very busy weekend on my part. Having to call each of you for a report over the phone. I don't like to disturb you on the weekend any more than I like to take the time to call each of you.

MEMO 3
TO: James Huang, Relocation Manager
FROM: Karen Mendes, V.P.
DATE: February 12, 2001
SUBJECT: Timeline for developing a relocation brochure

When we were together at our last meeting we outlined the contents of a brochure we will develop for employees relocating to the Fallsview Plant. Since then at our meeting I have learned that a major hiring effort will begin in september of this year, we need to have our brochure ready to enhance that effort. According to our printer the finished copy must be delivered to him by June 1 in order for him to return proof pages to us by July 15. If we are able to proofread and return the pages by July 30 he will promise the completed brochure by September 1.

Tell me the following: When will your dept. be free to work on the brochure full time? How many additional staff will you need for this project. How soon may I see your first draft?

Give me your answers at our Monday morning meeting.

PRACTICE 7

Correct the following report. Look for spelling, punctuation, and grammar errors. Simplify the sentences whenever you can. In brief, apply all that you have learned about effective communication.

Report to Stockholders

Comparing our company's productivity to our Japanese counterpart, in the 1990s, it increased by 20 percent and, at the same time, in that period of time, Japan's production grew over 100 percent. Likewise our German competitors which had productivity levels higher than ours were also less than Japan's. Still we must remember that although our industry still has the highest productivity in the world. Other countries, however, and especially Japan, has gained in productivity so consistantly every year so that by the end of the 1990s these foreign rivals were now in a position to invade our markets and they took away a lot of our business. They did this by beating us not only in price but also their quality has been consistently better.

Can Universal Widget corporation reverse this trend between 2000 and 2010? Your Board of Directors thinks it is capable of doing so. Universal Widget corporation has adapted a leadership position in research and development which will allow us to innovate, it will bring the newest and most advanced widget to the marketplace. In addition, because our plants are completely computerized, they are able to bring our product to the market place faster and it's also a better product.

Writing Practice

Before you begin writing, review the five steps to good writing.

Steps to Good Writing

1. **Plan:** Define topic and major point.
   Determine scope of writing.
2. **Outline:** Think through writing from beginning to end.
   Outlining serves to order thoughts and ideas and to subordinate supporting details to major points.
   A perfect, final outline is not necessary.
3. **Draft:** *Fast and furious.* Get it down on paper.
   Don't agonize over grammar, structure, mechanics, or word choice.
4. **Edit:** Fine tune. Now is the time to agonize over grammar, structure, mechanics, and word choice.
5. **Rewrite:** Produce the final product. Make sure that editing did not destroy the flow of writing. One change often necessitates others.
   Follow through.

The Editor's Checklist

Use the following checklist as a guide when editing your writing. First, review the personalized style sheet you started in Chapter 4. Use it as you review your writing.

Content:
_____Accurate
_____Clear
_____Concise

Format:
_____Subheadings
_____White space
_____Lists

Structure:
Each paragraph:
_____focuses on one topic
_____has a topic sentence
_____is limited to five or six sentences

Each sentence:
_____contains an average of 10 to 14 words
_____is well constructed
_____has clear terminology

Mechanics:

_____Correct grammar, punctuation, spelling

Personalized Style Sheet Cautions:

_____ _____

_____ _____

_____ _____

PRACTICE 8

Draft a one-page report on one of the following topics. Then, using the Editor's Checklist as your guide, edit your report and rewrite it.

1. The Value of Corporate Day-Care Centers
2. Addressing the Problems of the Homeless

ANSWERS

PRACTICE 1

1. Please *accept* my apology.
2. Jim doesn't want to argue. He said to *let* it be.
3. Ms. Atler did not intend her comments to *imply* that you were incompetent.
4. Please carry your résumé to the *Personnel* Department.
5. Any good report clearly states the *principal* issues.
6. Salad and fresh bread make a *healthful* lunch.
7. When Mr. Shen wants your *advice,* he will certainly ask for it.
8. When I have time for a break, I will *lie* down for a few minutes.
9. You *surely* don't think that I could type that quickly, do you?
10. This is a whole *other* topic.
11. I found last year's seminar more valuable *than* this year's.
12. Mr. Salle came *into* the meeting room 45 minutes late.
13. The choice for best composition is *among* these four. (One chooses *between two* items and from *among three* or more.)
14. There are *fewer* people in line for the 6:40 show than there are for the 8:40. (*Fewer* refers to number; *less* refers to amount.)
15. Many people are becoming concerned about the *effects* of air pollution on our health.
16. Ira is *eager* to see the new play.
17. José cannot find that position paper *anywhere.*
18. *It's* not too late to cancel the plane reservations.

PRACTICE 2

Answers will vary.

1. In this century, chemistry has played a part in studying the life sciences. As a result, research in chemistry has come together with research in other sciences. Increasing knowledge of chemical structures, for example, helps scientists understand basic life processes. This cooperation has resulted in biochemistry, brining together biology and chemistry.
2. At our last meeting, you asked for my thoughts on building your new plant in Clayton. To begin, your company would receive financial dividends by locating there since the corporate tax rate in Clayton is the lowest in the state. In addition, because everyone knows that Clayton is a fine place to live, you will have no trouble relocating employees to the area.
3. In the Louisiana Purchase of 1803, the United States obtained the title to Texas from France, and the Texas controversy took shape. The United States passed the title on to Spain in the Adams-Onis Agreement of 1819 in return for Florida. In the same year, Moses Austin was granted land from Spain to settle a colony in Texas. Austin's son, under a newly created Mexican government, independent of Spain, established a colony between the Brazos and Colorado rivers.
4. Public Relations Announcement
    The company's supervisor of operations states, "If a customer has a problem with our machinery, I receive the call. Through direct communication with our representatives all over the country, I can make the necessary deliveries and repairs. Our salespeople are like family. They are just as eager to effect the needed changes as we are. Customers appreciate that."
5. Existing curriculum does not always meet personal learning needs. The Adult College, therefore, offers students independent study. Students, then, have another option: to create a study program tailored to

their needs.

Because classes are held in the evening, students are still able to work at their jobs. In addition, students use their work as a laboratory, blending theory and practice under supervision and earning credit for their efforts.

PRACTICE 3
Answers will vary.

When I read the want ads, I cut out those I was interested in and glued them to index cards. In response to these ads, I called or sent my résumé. Usually, the eye-catching ads that offered the highest starting salaries involved sales work. As I learned in high school, however, that's not something I enjoy doing.

One job I really wanted was that of manager trainee in a book store. Part of the interview entailed a 30-page questionnaire. Question topics included corruption, drug abuse, employee theft, possible criminal record of the applicant, and, my personal favorite, "Do you have any bad habits?" Unfortunately, I could not think of any. Sometimes, I wonder if having bad habits would have gotten me the job.

PRACTICE 4
We have shown only the body of the letter here, with the corrections as you should have made them.

I *recently received* your package and must say I was *extremely* disappointed. You had promised me a *quality* product and I received an *inferior* one. How can such a well-known company *appear* to be reputable and yet make such an unreliable item? I respectfully *request* a refund.

PRACTICE 5
LETTER 1

1409 Grange Lane
San Francisco, California 90042
June 30, 2000

Mr. Martin Rivera
Well-Built Construction Company
21 Warren Road
San Francisco, California 90042

Dear Mr. Rivera:

You were highly recommended by my neighbor, but I fail to see why. A three-day project ended up taking two weeks. Your workmen left my yard a shambles after building a garage for me. I asked the men to clean up their garbage, but they refused. Please have someone from Well-Built complete this clean-up within the next five days. Thank you.

Sincerely,
Wilma Jones

LETTER 2
Answers will vary.

27 Main Street
Smalltown, USA 00000
April 2, 2000

Arthur Johnson
Superintendent of Schools
110 Pine Street
Smalltown, PA 10001

Dear Superintendent Johnson:

I read your report to the school committee on raising eligibility standards for high school athletes, and I disagree. Since other students can pass from grade to grade with a 1.5 average, how fair is it to insist that athletes maintain a 3.0 average? A student can move from grade 9 to 13, but he can't play football.

I agree that the first job of any student should be academic work. You can't declare, however, that only students with a 3.0 average can participate in sports, because that requirement doesn't take into account the needs or abilities of special students. In addition, a student's educational experience should be as complete as possible. The interaction that takes place in sports is a part of that experience. Please reconsider your position.

Sincerely,
Melvin Appley

LETTER 3
Answers will vary.

GILBEY CONSTRUCTION COMPANY
180 Main Street   Wethersfield, Kansas 66614

November 21, 2000

Mr. Steven Perl, President
Perfect Product Company
Lubbock, Texas 79403

Dear Steve:

Thank you for sending us your informative product brochure regarding partitions. While we think this is the product we need, we still have a few questions for you:

1. Can this model be mounted directly onto a ceramic floor?
2. Do you make a PVC partition in peach?
3. How much space do your partitions require?
4. How quickly can you deliver?

Please fax your response as soon as possible along with warranty information.

Sincerely,
Martin Morez

PRACTICE 6
MEMO 1
TO: Laura Perez, Sales Manager
FROM: Chaya Cohen, New Product Development Coordinator
DATE: December 19, 2001
SUBJECT: 2002 Annual Sales Conference

I am assembling my presentation to the sales representatives, but I find I will need some audiovisuals. Can you get me a large screen, a slide projector, and a lighted pointer? Also, the sound system at last year's conference was inadequate for the size room we had. Will you be able to improve on that this time? Let's meet about two weeks before the conference and go over the points I will be covering, in case you have some particular products you want to cover in depth.

MEMO 2
TO: All Department Heads
FROM: Bill Morrisey
DATE: January 12, 2001
SUBJECT: Weekly progress reports

As you know, I meet with Mr. Smith and Mr. Torres every Monday morning to give them a weekly progress report of all departments. When I don't receive your reports by Friday, I have to use the weekend to call each of you for the report. I don't like to disturb you on the weekend any more than I like to take the time to call you. I would appreciate your cooperation in getting these reports to me on time.

Notice the addition of the last sentence. Always state what you want your reader to do.

MEMO 3
TO: James Huang, Relocation Manager
FROM: Karen Mendes, Vice President
DATE: February 12, 2001
SUBJECT: Timeline for developing a brochure for relocating employees

At our last meeting, we outlined the contents of a brochure we will develop for employees relocating to the Fallsview plant. Since our meeting, I've learned that a major hiring effort will begin in September of this year; we need to have our brochure ready to enhance that effort. According to our printer, the finished copy must be delivered to him by June 1 in order for him to return proof pages to us by July 15. If we are able to proofread and return the pages to the printer by July 30, he will promise the completed brochure by September 1.
Please let me know the following:
1. When will your department be free to work on the brochure full time?
2. How many additional staff will you need for this project?
3. How soon may I see your first draft?
Please give me your answers at our Monday morning meeting.

PRACTICE 7
Answers may vary.
Report to Stockholders
In the 1990s, our company's productivity increased 20 percent in comparison to our Japanese counterpart's increase of over 100 percent. In the same years, our German competitor's productivity, while less than

the Japanese, also increased more than ours. Although our industry still maintains the highest productivity in the world, our foreign competitors have shown more consistent gains each year. By the end of the 1990s, therefore, our foreign rivals had invaded our markets and taken away a substantial amount of our business, beating us not only in price, but also in quality.

Can Universal Widget Corporation reverse the trend between 2000 and 2010? Your Board of Directors thinks the company is capable of doing so. Universal Widget Corporation has adopted a leadership position in research and development that will allow us to innovate, brining the most advanced widget to the marketplace. In addition, our newly computerized plant can produce a better widget and can bring it to the marketplace faster.

PRACTICE 8
Here are examples of the edited and rewritten reports. Answers will vary.
1. THE VALUE OF CORPORATE DAY-CARE CENTERS

The workforce has changed drastically in recent decades and will continue to change. More women work full time; more families rely upon two incomes; more women return to work soon after childbirth. To retain qualified workers, many companies are assisting two-income families by providing day care. Both the employer and the employee benefit from this service.

Employer Benefits

When on-site day care is provided, workers' attendance records show an increase and tardiness records show a decrease. Because a major concern—their children—is being addressed, workers focus more fully on the tasks at hand. Women take less time off after childbirth or for childrearing, thus maintaining continuity and saving training and retraining dollars. On-site day care is a benefit that assists in retaining good workers. Morale improves because employees know that their employer cares about them and their families.

Employee Benefits

Since on-site day care allows women to return to work more quickly after childbirth, it helps them to maintain their income levels. Additionally, when an employee is out for too long, she may return at a disadvantage in terms of recent information or newly needed skills. Employees also have more personal time because they do not have to travel to and from distant day-care centers. Finally, employees do not have to research day-care facilities and attempt to assess their caliber.

Conclusion

By addressing one of employees' major concerns—their children—employers who provide a day care center create a more positive work environment, which leads to greater productivity. Employees benefit by being able to work and enjoy quality child care.

2. ADDRESSING THE PROBLEMS OF THE HOMELESS

The number of homeless people in the United States has continued to increase at an alarming rate. The problems of the homeless need to be addressed in order to prevent their numbers from growing even more. This report discusses circumstances that lead to homelessness, problems of the homeless, and recommended solutions.

Causes of Homelessness

Circumstances that lead to homelessness include job loss, poor job skills, sudden exorbitant expenses because of illness or other personal problems, and dependence on someone who falls into any of the preceding categories. Losing a job, for those with little or no money to fall back on, can lead to homelessness if living expenses—rent or mortgage payments, food, clothing, utilities, and medical care—deplete savings. Those with poor job skills may not be able to support themselves or their families without public assistance. If they do not qualify for such assistance, or do not know how to obtain it, they can end up on the street. Additionally, skilled workers whose job markets are saturated may deplete all available resources. Separated or divorced women, especially those with children, may be victims, too. If these women have no job training or experience, they do not have the employment skills necessary to support themselves and their children.

Problems of the Homeless

The homeless face a multitude of problems. Precarious living conditions may subject them to violent crimes or expose them to the elements. They suffer from poor nutrition because there is inadequate money for proper food. The conditions are unsanitary, exposing the homeless to disease. Children growing up without a home may not see the positive aspects of our culture and, therefore, may become alienated from the mainstream of American life. Also, these children will not receive the education or job experience necessary to escape this way of life.

Recommended Solutions

The circumstances that lead to homelessness must be addressed to break the pattern. Job-training programs must be instituted and/or expanded in schools, communities, and businesses. These programs should be inexpensive and easily accessible. Since poor job skills are often the result of inadequate education, schooling should be available for those who need it.

The homeless must be made aware of agencies that can help them obtain employment, education, health care, and nutritional information and assistance. To accommodate the current homeless population, shelters and outreach programs must be expanded.

Conclusion

Existing programs must be expanded, and new programs implemented where necessary. Homelessness, however, will not be stemmed only by serving those now in need. The root causes must be addressed.

Resources

The American Heritage Dictionary of the English Language, New College Edition. Boston: Houghton Mifflin, 1994.

Bernstein, Theodore M. *The Careful Writer: A Modern Guide to English Usage.* New York: Atheneum, 1973.

Blumenthal, Lassor. *Successful Business Writing.* New York: Grosset & Dunlap, 1985.

Booher, Dianna D. *Communicate with Confidence: How to Say It Right the First Time Every Time.* New York: McGraw-Hill, 1994.

Brusaw, Charles T., Gerald J. Alred, and Walter E. Oliu. *The Business Writer's Handbook,* 5th ed. New York: St. Martin's Press, 1997.

Burchfield, R. W., ed. *The New Fowler's Modern English Usage,* 3rd ed. New York: Clarendon Press, 1996.

Cazort, Douglas. *Under the Grammar Hammer.* Los Angeles: Lowell House, 1997.

Diamond, Harriet, and Phyllis Dutwin. *English the Easy Way,* 3rd ed. Hauppauge, N.Y.: Barron's Educational Series, Inc., 1996.

Diamond, Harriet, and Phyllis Dutwin. *Grammar in Plain English,* 3rd ed. Hauppauge, N.Y.: Barron's Educational Series, Inc., 1997.

Dumaine, Deborah. *Write to the Top: Writing for Corporate Success.* New York: Random House, 1989.

Elsbree, Langdon, and Frederick Bracher. *Heath's Brief Handbook of Usage,* 9th ed. Boston: D.C. Heath & Co., 1977.

Flesch, Rudolph, and Salvatore Raimondo. *How to Write, Speak and Think More Effectively.* New York: New American Library, 1994.

Follett, Wilson. *Modern American Usage: A Guide.* Edited and completed by Jacques Barzun and others. New York: Hill & Wang, 1998.

Godden, Nell, and Erik Palma, eds. (Princeton Review). *Grammar Smart: A Guide to Perfect Usage.* New York: Villard Books, 1993.

Hochheiser, Robert M. *Throw Away Your Résumé!* 3rd ed. Hauppauge, N.Y.: Barron's Educational Series, Inc., 1995.

A Manual of Style, 14th ed., rev. Chicago: University of Chicago Press, 1993.

Mersand, J., and F. Griffith. *Spelling the Easy Way,* 2nd ed. Hauppauge, N.Y.: Barron's Educational Series, Inc., 1996.

Oliu, Walter E., Charles T. Brusaw, and Gerald J. Alred. *Writing That Works,* 6th ed. New York: St. Martin's Press, 1997.

The Random House Dictionary of the English Language, unabridged rev. ed. New York: Random House, 1989.

Strunk, William, and E.B. White. *The Elements of Style,* 3rd ed. Boston: Allyn and Bacon, 1979.

Turabian, Kate L. *A Manual for Writers of Term Papers, Theses, and Dissertations,* 6th ed. Chicago: University of Chicago Press, 1996.

The U.S. Government Printing Office Style Manual, rev. ed. 1986.

Wilson, Robert F., and Adele Lewis. *Better Résumés for Executives and Professionals,* 3rd ed. Hauppauge, N.Y.: Barron's Educational Series, Inc., 1996.

PRACTICE 9

Correct these sentences.

1. Businessmen and educators met to discuss the work-study program.

2. Every participant should meet the bus at his or her hotel.

3. Every reporter returned to his or her newspaper office.

4. We expect a salesman to call on our office monthly.

5. At full capacity, our company employs four repairmen.

PRACTICE 10

Correct the language problems in the following paragraph:

In reference to our business plan, I cannot emphasize enough that developing a business plan is not simply a technique to keep our finance department informed. The fact is that, in order to sell this company, we're going to have to show perspective buyers the direction in which we would take the company in the next five years. For example, our buyer has the right to know about our new product plans as well as our strategies to maximize our bottom line.